Representatives, Roll Calls, and Constituencies

Representatives, Roll Calls, and Constituencies

Morris P. Fiorina
California Institute of Technology

Lexington Books
D.C. Heath and Company
Lexington, Massachusetts
Toronto   London

Library of Congress Cataloging in Publication Data

Fiorina, Morris P.
   Representatives, roll calls, and constituencies.

   Bibliography: p.
   1. Representative government and representation—United States.
2. Political participation—United States. 3. Pressure groups—United States.
I. Title.
JK1071.F56   328.73'07'75   73-11647
ISBN 0-669-90217-9

Published simultaneously in Canada.

Printed in the United States of America.

International Standard Book Number: 0-669-90217-9

Library of Congress Catalog Card Number: 73-11647

To Mary and Michael

Contents

List of Figures

List of Tables

Preface

This book focuses on the question of constituency influence on representatives' roll call voting, a subject political scientists long have found interesting. But while traditional in topic this study is atypical in one respect: it is primarily analytical rather than empirical. For the most part the study examines the neat, precise world of theory, rather than the complex, ambiguous world of data. I am convinced that theoretical and empirical work must go hand in hand. And while many have studied constituency influence empirically, few have studied it theoretically.

The analysis which follows employs a smattering of mathematical argument, though nothing terribly fearsome. I have used mathematics to simplify, not obfuscate, to generate interesting (and hopefully true) substantive implications, not to play logical games. I stress these points only because occasionally the distinction is ignored.

I owe an incalculable debt to Professors William Riker, Richard Fenno, and Arthur Goldberg. I also thank a number of colleagues who have read, criticized, and otherwise commented on the work. They include Professors Kenneth Shepsle, David Rohde, Peter Wissel, Michael Coveyou, John Aldrich, John Ferejohn, Roger Noll, Robert Bates, Charles Plott, David Grether, John Jackson and others too numerous to mention. Because their advice was not always consistent, I have been unable to heed all of it. Therefore, I absolve them of most (but not all) of the blame, and, as usual, offer them most (but not all) of the credit. I also thank Mrs. Barbara Yandell for her patience, time, and labor in preparing the manuscript, and the Division of the Humanities and Social Sciences of Caltech for making available much-needed research assistance. Finally I thank my lovely wife, Mary, to whom I have promised any royalties this book earns. May my promise not be worthless.

1

Representatives, Roll Calls, and Constituencies

Introduction

The writings of democratic theorists reflect a long-standing general concern: how do the governed influence the councils of the governors? This book, too, reflects that concern. Of specific interest to us is the extent to which the roll-call voting records of representatives result from consideration of the opinions of their constituents. Thus, our concern is with the classical problem of representation. But we shall not engage in the continuing normative and semantic arguments about the meaning of "representation."[1] Rather, we simply will examine the relationship between a representative's votes and his constituents' preferences in a particular institutional setting, namely, U.S. federal, state, and local legislative bodies.

Our research focus removes from the study some areas of traditional concern. Because we examine the relationship between a single agent and a single district, we shall not consider the notions of the responsible parties advocates.[2] These scholars contend that representatives should vote as a united party which the electorate must judge as a whole. Nor will we consider the ideas of the classical thinkers on representation, whose works focus primarily on the aforementioned normative concerns. While important, ideas such as "general will" and "public interest" will not be discussed. Rather, we pose a set of deceptively simple empirical questions: "Who gets represented?" "Why?" "How much?" Attempts to answer these questions constitute the mainstream of contemporary research on constituency influence. Thus, we are not unusual in our choice of questions. But our method of proposing answers to these questions departs from the ordinary in that this study is primarily analytical rather than empirical. Although we certainly rely on numerous studies by empirically-oriented researchers, our major effort is an examination of the voting decisions of model legislators through applications of the theory of decision making. To the extent that our assumptions capture the crucial aspects of empirical legislative arenas, we expect the theoretical results to describe the voting behavior of real-life representatives. In the remainder of this chapter, we attempt to justify the choice of research strategy. This justification is best accomplished by means of a critical review of the literature on constituency and roll-call voting.

Too often, literature reviews are boring to author and reader alike. But if the reviewer does more than write a series of brief summaries, he can make a real contribution. Moreover, if one is willing to show a bit of contentiousness, critical reviews can be downright exciting.[3]

1

Most commonly one writes a literature review in order to acquaint an audience with the state of knowledge in a field. Such an educational function is the first purpose of our review. A second purpose is to demonstrate that we are not chasing a ghost—that constituents do exert some influence on their representative's voting. Periodically, large numbers of United States citizens become rather cynical about the actual working of "representative" government. The late 1960s and early 1970s appear to be such a period. Thus, some might charge that theories of constituency influence are vacuous—"elegant models of irrelevant worlds." If the literature supports such a contention, perhaps we should quit now.

If the literature shows that constituency influence is not altogether mythical, however, then our review serves a third purpose: it suggests questions, concepts, and relationships which we might take into account when constructing our theories. Those who read standard philosophy of science texts literally might blanch at the suggestion that empirical research may suggest theory rather than vice versa. But certainly, one would be foolish to ignore empirical findings when formulating one's theories. Finally, a critical review justifies the theoretical direction this work takes. Although many individual studies have merit, taken as a whole the literature is noncumulative, noncomparable, confusing, and sometimes simply contradictory. Much of the confusion disappears upon careful examination of the literature, but one should consider why it arises in the first place. We argue that the basic problem is the lack of theoretical underpinning for the research that has been done. In the final section of this chapter we elaborate on this contention. Meanwhile, let us proceed to a critical examination of empirical research. At present, what do we know about the relationship between constituents' preferences and their representatives' voting? On what knowledge can one build?

The Existence of Constituency Influence

Conveniently, the first major study to examine constituency influence on legislative voting raises directly the fundamental question of the existence of constituency influence. We refer, of course to Julius Turner's *Party and Constituency: Pressures on Congress.*[4] Turner presented masses of data from which it seemed reasonable to infer the existence, if not the primacy, of constituency influence. Using measures of foreign-born-native, urban-rural, and section as extremely crude surrogates for constituents' policy preferences, Turner showed that Congressmen divided along these lines, although not as often nor as deeply as along party lines. This latter finding is not terribly surprising, given the relatively greater precision of the party variable vis-à-vis the measures of constituency interest. Moreover, Wayne Shannon makes the important point that Turner's data cannot tell us much about the comparative strengths of party and constituency because the two are closely related.[5] Thus, if one controls for party, one may assign to party much variance that legitimately belongs to constituency.[6] Although we believe Shannon's remark is very well taken, most researchers have interpreted Turner's work as evidence for the primacy of party over constituency as an influence on Congressional voting behavior.

In addition to showing that Congressmen divide along sectional, ethnic, and urban-rural lines, Turner shows that constituency characteristics help explain variations in party loyalty. For example, the most impressive evidence for the existence of constituency influence which Turner presents lies in the overall portrait of the effects of the New Deal realignment. In the Congresses of 1921 and 1931, Turner found that Southern Democrats from rural, native-stock districts were the most loyal to their party, as were Northern Republicans from metropolitan districts to theirs. Conversely, in the Congresses of 1937 and 1944, the Southern native rural Democrats had become insurgents as had the metropolitan Northern Republicans. One can account for these observations by noting that the loci of the pre-1932 Democratic and Republican Congressional parties were the Southern Representatives and the Northern urban Representatives respectively, while the loci of the post-1932 parties were the urban Northern Democrats and rural mid-Western Republicans.[a] In simpler terms when the formerly atypical constituency type became the modal constituency type, and vice versa, the former insurgents became loyalists and the former loyalists became insurgents. This fact seems to indicate that when the program of the Congressional party changes, the members' constituencies exert a substantial drag on their ability to change with it. If party were everything and constituency pressure nothing, there would be little reason for loyalists and· insurgents to trade positions following a shift in the program of their party. A remarkable coincidence of enduring personal political beliefs provides the only other plausible explanation for a set of representatives refusing to follow a changed party program. And, given the volume of writings on the nonideological character of American politicians, it seems unlikely that personal beliefs could account completely for the tendency of groups of party loyalists to fail to rally to the newly emplaced party banner.[7]

In sum, we find the reasoning of Turner and Schneier quite plausible:

If a representative casts a large number of votes against his party, his record probably indicates the existence of some other source of behavioral cues, a pressure from outside sources operating against party pressure. If we find that representatives of particular kinds of districts vote against the party more often

[a]Regarding the pre-New Deal Democrats, Representative Richard Bolling writes:

What of the Democrats during the twelve-year period of Republican domination in the House extending from 1919 to 1931? During that period, its Southern wing *was* the Democratic party. In 1921, for example, 99 out of 134 Democrats, or 74 percent, were Southerners; the following year, 109 of 207; in 1929, 101 of 190; and in 1933, a total of 109 out of 219 . . . " (Italics in the original)

See Bolling's *Power in the House* (New York: Dutton, 1968), p. 115.

than representatives of other kinds of districts, it should be safe to identify such district pressures as a source of intraparty division.[8]

A number of succeeding studies have employed the basic research design introduced by Turner. To some extent they have sought to go beyond him by inferring relative strengths of constituency influence as well as its existence. Unfortunately, questionable inferences in some of these studies have produced considerable confusion in the literature.

In a classic study of the Massachusetts House of Representatives, Duncan MacRae, Jr., attempted to replicate and extend Turner's findings.[9] Using "key" votes from each of the sessions examined (1931-1932, 1941, 1951), MacRae constructed rough indices of party regularity. Similarly to Turner he finds that representatives from districts "atypical" of their legislative party are the least loyal to the party, where typicality is measured by the district percentage of owner-occupied dwellings (typical Democratic districts—low; typical Republican districts—high). Henceforth, we refer to this finding as the *atypicality hypothesis*.

MacRae proposed an interesting additional hypothesis with his suggestion that representatives may differ predictably in their susceptibility to constituency influence. Specifically, might a high degree of electoral competition "sensitize" a representative to constituents' preferences? MacRae finds that just as representatives from atypical districts tend to be least loyal to their party, so legislators from marginal, or competitive districts tend to be disloyal, in apparent support of his hypothesis. Henceforth we refer to this latter finding as the *marginality hypothesis*. The atypicality and marginality hypotheses are not independent, however, since atypical districts tend to be marginal, and vice versa.[b] MacRae suggests that

---

[b]One should note that MacRae attempted to control for the common effects of atypicality and marginality, concluding that each had an independent impact. We would contest this conclusion, however, for MacRae encounters the usual problem in attempting to control for the independent effects of two closely-correlated variables: some cells are thinly populated, even empty. MacRae looked separately at Democrats and Republicans in three sessions—six cases. For the 1951 session even the general finding that deviation increases with atypicality and marginality is not supported by the data; therefore, we concentrate on the four cases of the 1931-32 and 1941 sessions. For the Democrats in both sessions, deviation is quite high in the atypical range of percent O.O.D., but there exist *only* marginal districts in this range. That is, there are no *safe and atypical* districts with which to compare the *marginal and atypical* districts. In the more typically Democratic ranges of percent O.O.D., the differences between the average deviation of representatives from marginal and safe districts are very small and in several cases inconsistent with the hypothesis. Similarly, for the Republicans in the two sessions the differences between the deviation percentages of safe and marginal representatives are slight and not always consistent with the hypothesis in the moderate to high ranges of percent O.O.D. (typical Republican), although impressive differences exist in the low range (atypical Republican). But, as MacRae admits, there is a problem with the latter comparisons. The measure of percent O.O.D. " . . . groups a few Republican high-status district, such as Brookline, in the same classification with the solidly Democratic urban district." Thus, at the only data points where marginality appears to have

Those who wish to influence representatives in a direction different from the inclinations of their districts may have most success with those representatives who are in least danger of defeat at the next election. Those who wish to influence representatives toward the inclinations of their districts will probably be most successful with representatives who are in some danger of defeat at the next election.[10]

First of a number of attempted replications of MacRae is Dye's study of the 1958 Pennsylvania Legislature.[11] Dye succeeded in replicating MacRae's findings for the Pennsylvania House. Democrats' constituencies typically were urban and low income, and Republicans' constituencies typically rural and high income. The correlation between scores on a party deviation index and ruralism was .56 for Democrats and −.37 for Republicans, supporting the atypicality hypothesis. Electoral margin and deviation correlated moderately, −.46 for Democrats, and −.44 for Republicans, apparently supporting the marginality hypothesis. Dye pointed out that the areas of greatest electoral competition were those districts in which typically Republican socioeconomic characteristics balanced typically Democratic characteristics. Surprisingly, Dye found no relationship between demographic or competition variables and deviation in the smaller Pennsylvania Senate. In that body cohesion was uniformly high. To explain this discrepancy Dye recalled Madisonian arguments about the liberating effects of large, heterogeneous constituencies and long terms. Interestingly, in a study of the 1959-60 sessions of 26 state Senates, Le Blanc reported for Pennsylvania a multiple correlation of .64 between two socioeconomic variables (percent nonwhite, percent foreign stock) and support for the Democratic Senate majority.[12] Le Blanc's findings must be interpreted cautiously, however, because he did not control for party. Thus, properly or improperly, his correlations reflect the fact that high nonwhite and foreign stock districts tend to elect Democratic Senators who tend to vote Democratic.

Patterson found that Wisconsin "mavericks" (Republican violators of the norm requiring party unity on platform and procedural issues) came preponderantly from "close" districts and perceived their districts as closely contested and atypical of Republican districts.[13] In a later study of voting in the 1959 Oklahoma House, a one-party legislature, Patterson reports that members from competitive districts had higher *governor* support scores than those from safe districts.[14] This latter finding is difficult to interpret or compare with the previous findings regarding marginality and *legislative party* support.

---

an important impact independent of atypicality, one might actually be viewing the differences between marginal Republicans from *atypical* districts and safe Republicans from what are actually *typical* districts. In view of these considerations we are unwilling to conclude as MacRae did, " . . . that the political contest in a constituency has a distinct effect, over and above the socio-economic characteristics." Still, we would credit MacRae with a determined attempt to sort out the effects of atypicality and marginality. Subsequent research seldom has addressed the question. One exception, Wayne Shannon, also runs afoul of small cell sizes in crucial comparisons. See ref. note 5, pp. 163-166.

Using an analysis of variance technique Flinn found that constituency demographic variables were related to party voting in the 1959 Ohio Senate.[15] But, in contrast to earlier work, he concluded that "Electoral margins seem to have little to do with loyalty to party, except that the least secure members of the legislature, i.e., the members of the winning party with lowest pluralities, are less likely to be loyal than other members."[16]

A decade after MacRae's original study Pesonen attempted to replicate the atypicality and marginality hypotheses for the 1961 Massachusetts House.[17] Percent owner-occupied dwellings appeared to have lost much of its discrim- inatory value—most Republican districts fell in the medium range on that variable rather than the high range as in MacRae's study. But there still appeared to be a relationship between atypicality and deviation. The most surprising of Pesonen's findings was that a rather strong relationship between marginality and deviation existed among Democrats, but among Republicans the relationship was weak and in the opposite direction. That is, the Republicans from safe districts were slightly more likely to deviate than were those from close districts.

Finally, Parsons reports that in one-party Florida, representatives from Southern districts undergoing socioeconomic change (and growing Republican strength) increasingly find themselves in opposition to former allies from unchanging Northern districts.[18] Using longitudinal data Parsons shows that Southerners increasingly have opposed Northerners to the point where majorities from each section are now in opposition on fully half the "controversial" roll calls.

The findings thus far discussed seem intuitively acceptable. As Crane and Watts comment:

One plausible hypothesis is that legislators from more competitive districts will tend to be locally oriented because their re-election depends in large measure on their satisfying local demands. Legislators from competitive districts, knowing that their party label alone will not assure them of re-election, must be more concerned about the specific interests of their districts; but legislators from one-party districts are in less danger from the opposition and can concern themselves with a broader state interest.[19]

Since atypical districts tend to be marginal the argument applies as well to representatives from atypical districts. Still, one cannot elevate the atypicality and marginality hypotheses to the status of empirical generalizations. For one thing, as might be expected from Dye's study, these relationships do not seem to hold with any consistency in the Congress. Regarding the atypicality hypothesis, Froman finds that Democrats from "conservative" districts and Republicans from "liberal" districts (i.e., districts whose socioeconomic characteristics are associated with liberal or conservative attitudes) have lower and higher Kennedy Support scores respectively, than their colleagues from typical districts.[20] But other data he reports show little if any relation between constituency characteristics and voting behavior.[21] After extensive data analysis Shannon concludes that " . . . both Democrats and Republicans from very atypical constituencies are little if any less loyal (or less typical in terms of policy choice) than other members of their party."[22]

Regarding the marginality hypothesis, the results of Congressional research are similarly inconclusive. Shannon found a slight relationship between party defection and marginality among Democrats in the 86th and 87th Congresses.[23] But most of this relationship was produced by the voting of those Democrats who came from normally Republican rather than simply competitive districts. For the Republicans the relationship is somewhat stronger.[24] In the 87th Congress Froman finds that for the Republicans, Partisan Support and Party Unity increase with safety, but the *most competitive* districts (farm districts) are also quite loyal.[25] For the Democrats Froman finds no relationship.

Now, at first glance it would appear that at least in state legislatures we have learned something about the *extent* of constituency influence as well as its mere existence. Namely, marginal representatives heed constituents' wishes more so than safe representatives. The mixed evidence from Congressional studies is troubling but not critical. We are stymied, however, when another Congressional study is examined. Warren Miller's "Majority Rule and the Representative System of Government" forces us to reexamine the ground just covered.[26]

Miller arrives at such unexpected conclusions as these:

. . . Congressmen from marginal districts are much more likely to translate their policy preferences directly into roll call behavior than are Congressmen from the safe districts; and we shall note that translation results in much less policy agreement than exists between constituents and Congressmen in one-party districts.

It is the marginal district Congressmen who virtually ignore what they think to be district preferences in favor of their personal attitudes on policy questions—and this by a spectacular margin . . .

Legislative acts of Congressmen from competitive districts are associated almost exclusively with their own policy preferences rather than with their perceptions of district preferences. The behavior of Congressmen from safe districts reflects a more even balance between the two factors, but their perceptions of constituency policy positions are clearly more highly related to their roll call decisions than are their personal policy attitudes.[27]

Let us examine the basis for Miller's inferences. His research design differs considerably from the early Turner design. Rather than use party loyalty scores as a dependent variable, Miller uses scores on three issue scales: social welfare (SW), civil rights (CR), and foreign policy (FP), and instead of constituency demographic or electoral characteristics as independent variables, Miller uses actual constituent attitudes obtained through surveys. In Figure 1-1 we illustrate Miller's data for the civil rights area.

Evidently, Miller's analysis yields results which are perplexing, to say the

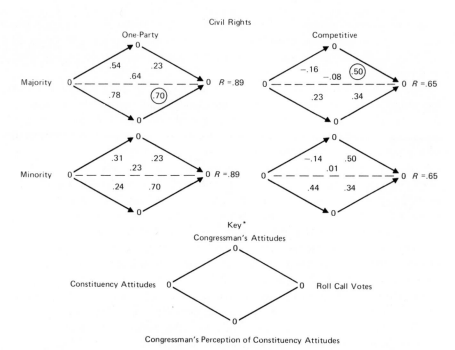

Figure 1-1. The Miller Data for Civil Rights. Source: Warren Miller, "Majority Rule and the Representative System of Government," in E. Allardt and Stein Rokkan (eds.), *Mass Politics* (New York: Free Press, 1970), pp. 300-301. *The numbers placed between constituency attitudes and Congressman's attitudes, Congressman's votes and Congressman's perceptions of constituency attitudes are simple Pearson r's. The numbers between Congressman's attitudes and roll call votes and Congressman's perceptions and roll call votes, are standardized regression coefficients estimated by assuming the Congressman's vote is a function of his attitudes and perceptions. *R* is the multiple correlation obtained from that estimation.

least. One sees first that there exists much *greater agreement* between majority constituents and their Representatives' voting in safe than in competitive districts: .64 vs. −.08. Second, one notes that Representatives from safe districts perceive the attitudes of their constituents more accurately than do Representatives from marginal districts: .78 vs. .23. Third, one sees that Representatives from safe districts are much more likely *to vote their perceptions of constituency attitudes* than are Representatives from marginal districts: .70 vs. .34. On the contrary, Representatives from marginal districts are more likely *to vote their own attitude* than are those from safe districts: .50 vs. .23. Given these findings and comparing them to MacRae's earlier conclusion we face a stark contradiction.

MacRae asserted explicitly that representatives from marginal districts are more subject to constituency influence than their colleagues from safe districts. Yet Miller's findings just as explicitly indicate the opposite. Obviously, there are ways to pass off the contradiction, but none of them are very satisfactory.

One can dismiss Miller's small constituency samples as unreliable. Still, the findings are consistent over all three issue areas, and quite strong in the areas of social welfare and civil rights. One can point out that MacRae studies a state legislature while Miller studied Congress. But while it is logically possible that electoral marginality affects state legislators exactly oppositely from the manner in which it affects Congressmen, one would think that possibility exceedingly unlikely. Such a disparity between the national and state legislative worlds should be the last hypothesis considered, not the first. One might note the different independent and dependent variables in the conflicting studies. Even so, real-world regularities should not depend so completely on our choice of measures. No, there is no easy denying of the contradiction. Something is amiss. And that something would appear to be an unjustified inference in MacRae's study which succeeding researchers have failed to rectify. The crucial question is this: where does one find any basis for assuming that loyalty to one's party necessarily implies disloyalty to one's constituency, or alternately, that loyalty to one's constituency implies disloyalty to one's party? This assumption has no basis, but it is absolutely necessary to link the data from the MacRae study design to the conclusion that is drawn. Without it, the marginality hypothesis is a non sequitur.

MacRae defined "typical" Republican districts as those high on percent owner-occupied dwelling units and "typical" Democratic districts as those low on the same measure. This seemed a reasonable procedure, since as shown in Figure 1-2 the 1940 percentage of owner-occupied dwellings (O.O.D.) does appear to discriminate fairly well between (1951) Republican and Democratic districts. Note further, though, that percent O.O.D. discriminates even better between the safe Republican and safe Democratic seats, which constituted 65 percent of each party's seats. The bulk of the competitive seats fell in the intermediate range of percent O.O.D., the range not typical of either party. What we see from Figure 1-2 is that "typical" seats are defined by reference to the characteristics of safe seats.

It would seem that safe seat legislators are likely to constitute the core of most legislative parties. Given the general importance of experience, they often hold the leadership posts and chair the committees. Even if a strict seniority rule is not followed in a particular legislature, experience in playing the legislative game can usually be parlayed into influence. Furthermore, as in Massachusetts, safe-seat legislators probably are a majority of most legislative parties. What do these arguments suggest? Simply that the safe seat legislators are likely to have a disproportionate influence in setting the party line: to a great extent they *are* the legislative party. But this fact has crucial implications, for if safe seat

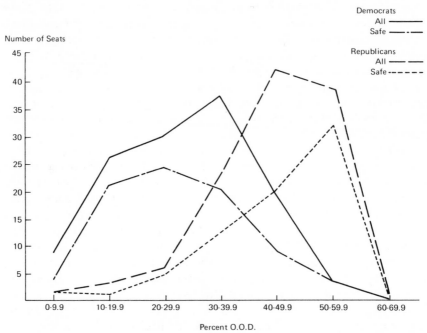

Figure 1-2. Distribution of Districts over Range of Percent O.O.D. (1951). Source: Adapted from Duncan MacRae, "The Relation between Roll-Call Votes and Constituencies in the Massachusetts House of Representatives," *American Political Science Review*, 46 (1952), p. 1047, p. 1049.

legislators come from similar constituencies, which was the case in Massachusetts and probably elsewhere, then hypothetically, they can set the party line while voting nothing but their constituents' preferences.[c] For those from safe, typical

---

[c]From this argument one can see why the marginality hypothesis usually applies more to Republicans than to Democrats in Congressional roll-call voting. There are two types of safe Democratic districts—Northern urban districts and Southern Districts—whose preferred policies are quite different. Thus, little possibility exists that the party line can or will coincide with the constituency interests of all safe-seat Democrats. Presumably the Democratic party line represents something of a compromise. Note that this argument is consistent with the general finding of David Mayhew's research. Mayhew concludes that the Congressional Democratic Party practices inclusive compromise: the constituency interests of minority elements in the party are not ignored in defining the party program. Conversely, the Republican Congressional Party practices exclusive compromise: the party program sacrifices the constituency interests of minority elements in the Party. Thus, if the minority, atypical districts are marginal, one would expect to find marginality related to deviation among Republicans, but not among Democrats. See David Mayhew, *Party Loyalty Among Congressmen* (Cambridge: Harvard University Press, 1966).

Additionally, we now can suggest the basis for Pesonen's unusual findings reported on page 9. Pesonen found that deviation and marginality were positively related among Democrats in the 1961 session of the Massachusetts Assembly, but not among Republicans (we compute gammas of .57 and −.14, respectively, from his tables). Why? From Pesonen's

districts constituency loyalty and party loyalty present no conflict. A highly significant but too little noticed finding is that 57 percent of Patterson's "mavericks" reported frequent district-party conflict, whereas only 23 percent of the regulars did.[28]

When investigators remark that the minority of representatives who come from competitive, atypical districts deviate from party positions more than the majority from safe, typical districts, what are they actually showing? They are showing that Republicans from Republican districts vote Republican, while those from not-so-Republican districts do so less frequently; and similarly for Democrats. Where in such an argument does one find any basis for concluding that the safe seat representatives are more likely to discount the preferences of constituents than are competitive seat representatives? So long as indices of party loyalty are employed as dependent variables, one can assert nothing about the strength of constituency influence on different representatives without supporting knowledge of the extent to which their party and their constituency interests clash.

The most surprising aspect of the twenty-year history of the marginality hypothesis is that the arguments just presented to attack that hypothesis are not new. Consider the following remarks of Malcolm Jewell:

If the members of a legislative party represent similar constituencies, the individual legislator is less likely to experience serious conflicts between the viewpoints of most of the legislators in his party and the views of dominant groups in his constituency. He is free from conflicting pressures and he finds it easy to go along when his party takes a stand on a bill . . .

In those state legislatures where the party represents a wide diversity of constituency interests, there is no basis for high party cohesion.[29]

And David Mayhew says it nicely:

It may plausibly be assumed that a bloc of Congressmen subjected to coinciding party and constituency pressures will demonstrate greater unity than a bloc subjected to conflicting pressures from party and constituency.[30]

Thus, elements of our argument appear in the literature, but students of constituency influence have never put them together, or at least they have not considered the full implications for the conclusions they drew. The contradiction which provoked this discussion need trouble us no longer, though MacRae's mistaken inference seems intuitively more plausible than Miller's valid one.

---

data the following facts emerge. In 1961 marginal Democratic districts were still atypical (gamma = .67), but marginal Republican districts were not (gamma = −.16). Republican districts were no longer differentiated at all well by the measure percent O.O.D. On the basis of these findings and the argument in the text we take this position: atypicality is a more fundamental variable than competitiveness. Where marginal seats are also clearly atypical, party deviation will be associated with marginality. Where typical and atypical districts are difficult to characterize (as in Congress) the relationship between party deviation and marginality will not appear. For an expansion on these remarks, see Chapter 5.

Overall, one must conclude that studies which employ various types of party unity scores as dependent variables provide very limited information about constituency influence. The finding that representatives from certain types of constituencies systematically deviate from party positions provides some justification for inferring the existence of constituency influence, but little else. To proceed further, other study designs are necessary.

The Extent of Constituency Influence

Advances in the study of constituency influence came with the adoption of new measures of legislative voting behavior. These measures in turn stemmed from the development of various scaling and clustering techniques.[31] Yet, it is unclear whether the greater precision afforded by such improved methods has produced a corresponding increase in our knowledge. Although scale studies have revealed many relationships between constituency characteristics and voting behavior, they have not provided a set of reliable empirical generalizations. To a great extent they have set us adrift on a sea of correlation coefficients.

MacRae's *Dimensions of Congressional Voting* merits the same classic status as Turner's *Party and Constituency*.[32] Using Guttman scaling MacRae confirmed the preliminary results of previous research.[33] No single liberal-conservative continuum could represent a Congressman's total voting record. Instead, a number of distinct dimensions, not identical between parties, appeared to underlie voting in the 81st Congress House of Representatives. MacRae constructed a Fair Deal scale for Democrats, components of which required two scales for the Republicans. Other scales included foreign aid, race relations, and agriculture. After placing Congressmen according to their positions along the scales, MacRae examined the relationships between scale scores and constituency characteristics such as percent farm workers, and urban-rural. Unfortunately, the myriad relationships he uncovered would require a rather long list. The best single summary statement one can make is the following: some constituency characteristics are weakly to moderately related to voting on some issue dimensions.[d]

Shannon's later scale study of the 86th and 87th Congresses House of Representatives further qualifies MacRae's findings: some constituency characteristics are weakly to moderately related to voting on some issue dimensions at some times.[34] Shannon did not replicate all of MacRae's earlier findings, and found some new ones besides. We will not list Shannon's numerous substantive findings either. Suffice it to quote the following discussion of Southern Democratic voting behavior to convey the sometimes extreme idiosyncratic flavor of the conclusions of scale studies.

---

[d]Because MacRae constructed separate scales for the two parties, he is unable to compare party influence vis-à-vis constituency influence. But within each party he can compare the relative importance of various constituency characteristics from issue to issue.

It can only be said that extreme southern Democratic conservatism is at times linked to rural and high nonwhite population, but at other times there would appear to be no relationship between these factors. In one case—aid to education—a relationship appears, but one that runs precisely counter to what might be expected from the hypothesis that rural, black belt southerners ought to be more conservative than those from urban and low nonwhite areas. Linkage between the constituency factors examined and voting behavior on the scales seems to shift from issue to issue. On policy matters involving housing, minimum wage, and foreign aid, rural and high nonwhite population are both clearly linked to conservatism. On the issue of welfare, only the influence of rural population is apparent. Both factors are weakly linked to southern conservatism on the issue of area redevelopment. On the other hand, in labor matters no voting differences were apparent during the Eighty-sixth Congress, despite the great constituency differences that characterized the southern Democratic delegation in the House. And finally, in the matter of aid to education both factors examined are *negatively* related to conservatism during one Congress and *positively* related during the other. To say the least, these results are extremely cryptic.[35]

MacRae, as would be expected, also tested a variant of the marginality hypothesis using scale scores as a dependent variable. Some relationships existed for Republicans but none for Democrats.[36]

Van Der Slik's 1969 study represents something of a departure from earlier studies in that he omits the party variable and allows constituency characteristics to account for as much of the total variance in voting as possible.[37] This procedure deserves a fair consideration. Because the Congressional parties each have their base in constituencies of a distinctive socioeconomic type, they themselves may be largely a reflection of constituency differences.[e] Thus, to control for party may be to weaken artificially the links between constituency and voting. Still, even using a procedure which gives constituency all the breaks, so to speak, Van Der Slik's findings are no more definitive than MacRae's and Shannon's. Correlating 21 constituency demographic characteristics with 12 issue scales yields a total of 252 Spearman rank order correlations. Only 19 of these correlations are greater than ± .4, while only 82 are greater than ± .25. The two dimensions most closely associated with constituency characteristics are Negro Rights and Agriculture Policy.

One of the most recent scale studies is Aage Clausen's ambitious examination of Congressional voting over a seventeen-year period.[38] Clausen found that in the 82nd to 88th, and the 91st Congresses, five major dimensions of voting were present: government management, social welfare, civil liberties, agricultural assistance, and international involvement. Except for a possible change in the international involvement dimension, these broad categories show a marked stability over time. Clausen attempts to assess the roles of party, constituency, ideology, and Presidential influence in Congressional voting. But although his study is often impressive, we find his examination of constituency influence baffling.

---

[e]Refer to reference note No. 5.

Clausen begins with the very appropriate observation that a representative's perceived constituency is not identical to the legally specified constituency. Whereas the latter includes all citizens of voting age in the district, the former might best be considered as " . . . the subset of voters who supported the representative in the last election. . . . Stated in the baldest terms, the implication of this discussion of constituency definitions is that legislators are expected to represent the subset of constituents who voted for them on the Big Day."[39] So far, so good. In seeking to measure constituency influence, however, Clausen contradicts his own view:

If party influence is effective in producing differences in policy positions, one would expect a partisan turnover in the representation of a constituency to produce a change in the policy representation provided. On the other hand, where constituency forces are dominant and partisan influence is nil, one would expect no change in policy representation when a particular seat in Congress passes from one party to the other.[40]

Clearly, we cannot accept such an argument. Certainly party influence would produce a change, but so would constituency influence. If a Democrat defeats a Republican in a given district, we surely don't suppose that they have the same constituency, that the differences in their voting stem from partisan influence alone. Clausen's reason for reverting to the legal definition of constituency is clear:

It would be inappropriate to the current analysis to use the more realistic definition of constituency, because this constituency changes with the occupancy of the seat, particularly in the condition of partisan turnover.[41]

Exactly. The legal definition of constituency is analytically convenient in that it enables Clausen to claim that constituency influence is held constant while representatives change. But in this case analytical convenience generates grievous substantive error. If one deliberately attempted to formulate a research design which confounded party and constituency as much as possible, one could not do better than Clausen's.

Clausen goes on to examine his data with the following questions in mind:

Is Congressional behavior highly stable over time as is expected where constituency influence is strong? Or is the policy representation of a constituency highly variable over time, thereby implying the weakness of constituency relative to other factors?[42]

Party change results in quite different voting on the government management, social welfare, and agricultural assistance dimensions, but not so much on civil liberties or international involvement. Thus, Clausen concludes that constituency influence is strongest on international involvement and important on civil liberties, while party dominates on the other three dimensions. Given our criticisms of Clausen's design, we believe the more appropriate conclusion would be that party *and* constituency are important on social welfare, government management, and agricultural assistance, while little can be said about constituency influence on civil liberties and international involvement. This conclusion may not be empirically correct, but it is the only one justified by the data.

In a later chapter Clausen also carries out an analysis along lines similar to that of MacRae.[43] Two district demographic variables—occupation and urbanization—are weakly related to Congressmen's policy positions on the five dimensions when all Representatives are considered. But as the predictive power of party weakens, the association between urbanization and voting behavior increases dramatically. Additionally, if the analysis is carried out within parties, the two demographic characteristics explain significant proportions of the variance in voting, particularly for Democrats.

Before moving on, one should note that Clausen's research also focuses on *State party* as a variable affecting Congressional voting.[44] Perhaps the "constituency" is broader than a Congressman's supporters in his district. Although still in its infancy, the study of state party potentially could shed further light on the nature of constituency influence.

Probably because of the finer research mesh, investigators of Congressional roll-call voting typically concentrate on the House rather than the Senate. Exceptions are Clausen and John Jackson. Jackson's work in particular provides an interesting contrast to the several scale studies just discussed. Given Senators' long terms and large districts, one might expect less of a relationship between state characteristics and Senate roll call voting than between district characteristics and House roll call voting. But no such implication follows from Jackson's work; quite the contrary.

In his first study Jackson constructed scales for the 1949 Public Housing, Reciprocal Trade, and Foreign Aid Bills, and the 1954 Foreign Aid and Excise Tax Cut Bills.[45] He conducted separate analyses for Republicans, Southern Democrats, and Northern Democrats on each of the five bills, using various combinations of 14 standard demographic variables as independent variables. The 15 multiple linear regressions resulted in an average r^2 (i.e., statistical variance explained) of 56 percent, with a range of 20 percent to 83 percent. Overall, Jackson was successful in explaining more of the variance on the domestic policy bills than on the foreign policy bills. Additionally, for Northern Democrats and Republicans, state characteristics accounted for more variance in voting when the party was out of power than when in power. This latter relationship was reversed for Southern Democrats. As in the MacRae, Shannon, and Van Der Slik Studies, however, particular variables related differently to roll call voting across issue scales and across the three groups of Senators.

Jackson's second study is more comprehensive and sophisticated than the first.[46] Moreover, he uses an ingenious procedure in developing his models. Rather than consider as a set of observations all Senators' scores on a single scale, Jackson defined a set of observations as a single Senator's scores on all the issue scales (36). Substantively, this presumes that a Senator weights the influences on his vote the same way on each issue, although the weights may differ from Senator to Senator. The standard method presumes the weights differ from issue to issue, but estimates the same weights for all Senators in each issue area. Jackson found his models statistically far superior to the standard models. Of more direct relevance, the constituency variable (which was estimated by a somewhat involved technique) proved to be the most consistently significant independent variable. Constituency was an especially good predictor variable for Republicans and Southern Democrats. Constituency was less important for the voting of Northern Democrats, for whom party and committee variables were relatively more important than for Southern Democrats and Republicans. Interestingly, Jackson's models perform as well for foreign policy issues as for domestic issues.

Scales represent an obvious improvement over indices of party loyalty as dependent variables. Just as obviously, however, room for improvement still exists in both dependent and independent variables, particularly the latter. A number of studies, quite disparate in design and focus, have introduced novel measures of constituency preferences. The findings of these studies are both interesting and encouraging.

In a substantive area notable for weak correlations between variables, unusually strong statistical relationships are reported in Flinn and Wolman's study of Southern Democratic voting behavior in the House of Representatives.[47] The dependent variables ranged from a policy variable—support for a Larger Federal Role, through a mixed policy-unity variable—Kennedy Support Score, to a straight unity variable—the *Congressional Quarterly* Party Unity Score. Of greater interest, however, Flinn and Wolman used constituency electoral characteristics other than marginality as independent variables. They employed the percent of the 1960 Kennedy vote and the percent of the 1948 States' Rights vote in each district as electoral variables. Demographic variables also were used in the analysis, but proved to be related to voting behavior less strongly than the electoral variables. All together, the variables used accounted for 29 to 57 percent of the statistical variance in the voting measures.

John Kessel's study of the Washington Congressional delegation contains a report of an impressive relationship between roll-call voting and constituency.[48] Kessel scored the Washington Representatives' voting favorability to a larger federal role in six policy areas. Then he compared these scores with the Representatives' perceptions of their districts' attitudes in the six areas. He found a τ_c of .69, indicating a close correspondence between perception of constituents' opinions and behavior. Kessel's study is the first reviewed in which subjective estimates of constituency opinion rather than more objective indicators serve as independent variables. The strength of the relationship he found augurs well for further research of this type.

Crane's study of the 1957 Wisconsin Legislature perhaps provides the most impressive single demonstration of constituency influence.[49] The dependent variable was the legislator's vote on a referendum proposal to institute Daylight Saving Time. Crane compared the votes of individual legislators with majority opinion in their districts as expressed by voting returns in the subsequent referendum. Eighty-five percent of the representatives voted consistently with the majority vote in their districts. Furthermore, Crane interviewed the Representatives to discern the basis of their vote and their perceptions of constituency opinion. He concluded that only three of eighty legislators *knowingly* voted against a majority of constituents. In some ways Crane's study is a model to be emulated. One cannot deny that the referendum results were probably a far better measure of constituency opinion than the standard demographic variables. Additionally, a legislator's vote on a single issue is a quite precisely defined dependent variable. Unfortunately, the conditions which make Crane's study design possible simply do not occur very frequently in the empirical world.

The studies of MacRae, Shannon, Van Der Slik, Jackson, Clausen, Flinn and Wolman, Kessel, and Crane all represent efforts to go beyond the Turner research design by use of dependent variables more specific in nature than party unity or loyalty. Yet we have seen that these studies, while enabling us to map more accurately the associations between constituency characteristic and roll-call voting, leave us as far as ever from the formulation of reliable generalizations. Indeed, Shannon appears to give up hope of the latter.[50] Of course there is one obvious improvement yet to be made. As mentioned, Flinn and Wolman, Kessel, and Crane all uncover quite strong relationships between constituency and vote. And, as we have seen, these studies make use of independent variables which capture more of a constituency than census data. How well does percent blue collar capture the policy preferences of a constituency? Certainly it is conceivable that a district containing 60 percent UAW members differs more from a district containing 60 percent nonunion Southern textile workers than it does from one containing 60 percent white collar workers. Are rural New York and rural Mississippi districts comparable? Possibly good sample survey data on constituents' preferences might solve our problems. If we knew the actual preferences of constituents on various issues, might the relationships between constituency and legislative roll-call voting appear much stronger and more stable than previously?

In 1958 the Survey Research Center of the University of Michigan conducted interviews with incumbent Congressmen, their opponents, and constituents in 116 Congressional districts. Since there were less than 2,000 constituents interviewed, the average number of interviews per average constituency of 410,000 is 17. While Miller and Stokes emphatically defend the accuracy of their data, one does seem justified in expressing skepticism that such small samples could provide a reliable basis for inferring constituents' preferences, especially when constituencies are later broken down into majority-minority sectors.[51]

Still, since these data are all that are available we will accept them as sound and consider the studies based on them. These number three published articles. Political scientists are most familiar with "Constituency Influence in Congress."[52] In that article Miller and Stokes report substantial agreement between constituents' attitudes and Congressmen's votes in the policy areas of Social Welfare and Civil Rights; product-moment correlations are .3 and .6, respectively. Granted, one may question whether correlations in the range .3 to .6 express "substantial agreement" between Representatives and constituents, especially since these estimates are based on averages of ordinal level data. One answer would appear to be that any relationships at all are more than expected given an earlier article by Stokes and Miller.

Stokes' and Miller's "Party Government and the Saliency of Congress" might go under the alias of "The Irresponsible Electorate."[53] In this paper Stokes and Miller paint a picture of an abysmally ignorant Congressional voter. Probably only half the electorate even knew which party controlled the 85th Congress. Only seven percent of the voters explained their votes by reference to legislative issues. The parties' legislative records were no better known to those who deviated from their party identification than to those who voted their party identification. In fact, fifty-four percent of the voters reported voting without having read or heard anything about either candidate. Stokes and Miller state that "Our constituent interviews indicate that the popular image of the Congressman is almost barren of policy content."[54] There we have it. Why should one expect to find constituency influence on Congressional voting? Constituents apparently don't care about Congressional issues.[f] What relationships one finds between constituency characteristics and roll-call votes must arise either because Congressmen are themselves somehow representative of the attitudes of the constituency, or because they attempt to anticipate what their somnolent masters might say if approached by an SRC interviewer.[g] Let us say

[f]Knowledge of the issues and voting based on that knowledge are not the only linkage conditions one might investigate in a study of constituency influence. John Sullivan and Robert O'Connor point out that we must also ascertain whether Congressional candidates offer the voters a choice and whether candidates vote consistently with their campaign positions. Utilizing roll-call data and candidates' responses to *Congressional Quarterly* questionnaires, Sullivan and O'Connor conclude that the two latter linkage conditions are satisfied. See their "Electoral Choice and Popular Control of Public Policy: The Case of the 1966 House Elections," *American Political Science Review* 64 (1972), pp. 1256-1268.

[g]A third possibility is suggested by Goldberg. He argues that there may exist a rational component to group norms such as party identification:

At least in retrospect, the notion is an obvious one. If one considers the origins of group norms, one expects that at their inception they were rational means to group ends. It may not then be surprising to find that they continue to be rational guides to action, even when learned on primarily affective bases.

Stokes and Miller report that in the 1958 election approximately 84 percent of the sample voted consistently with their party identification. Thus, even in the absence of mass constituency awareness a Representative may be indirectly influenced by the need to retain the nomination of the district party and to avoid primaries. See Arthur Goldberg, "Social Determinism and Rationality as Bases of Party Identification," *American Political Science Review*, 63 (1969), p. 21.

then, that the correlations between constituents' attitudes and Representatives' votes in the areas of Civil Rights and Social Welfare are greater than one might have anticipated from knowledge of the state of awareness of the constituency. Miller and Stokes found no relationship between constituents' attitudes and Representatives' votes in the area of foreign affairs.

Yet, despite the bleak picture of the constituency painted by Stokes and Miller, there remains a nagging problem. Namely, the Congressmen themselves do not accept the SRC picture:

Of our sample of Congressmen who were opposed for re-election in 1958, more than four-fifths said the outcome in their districts had been strongly influenced by the electorate's response to their records and personal standing. Indeed, this belief is clear enough to present a notable contradiction: Congressmen feel that their individual legislative actions may have considerable impact on the electorate, yet some simple facts about the Representative's salience to his constituents imply that this could hardly be true.[55]

Are we to believe that those who stake their careers on their political savvy could be so wrong?

The third SRC study already has been discussed in connection with the marginality hypothesis. Breaking down the data by the Congressman's perception of his district's competitiveness reveals that safe Congressmen to a great extent vote their perceptions of majority constituents' opinions. Marginal Congressmen do not. Presently we have no explanation for this finding. We will return to it later.

Let us summarize this section. A number of studies which improve on the Turner design have examined constituency influence in various issue areas. For the most part these studies report fairly weak relationships between constituency characteristics and voting behavior—relationships which fluctuate considerably over time. The separation of party from constituency influence still eludes us despite attempts to unravel it. Studies which get at representatives' perceptions of their constituencies and constituents' actual attitudes show stronger relationships between constituency and voting, although one of the latter studies yields a puzzling finding of its own: Congressmen secure in their electoral position follow fairly closely their perceptions of constituency preferences; Congressmen in tenuous electoral positions don't. In sum, extensive data analysis over a fairly long time period leaves us rich in our knowledge of specific statistical relationships, but poor in our ability to make general statements about constituency influence on legislative voting behavior.

Constituency and Electoral Strategy

Thus far we have considered a number of studies which attempt to provide a direct assessment of constituency influence. Questions such as the existence of constituency influence, its importance relative to other factors, and its variation across issue areas have received attention. In this section we will examine evidence offered as an answer to a different type of question. Some researchers have focused not on constituency influence per se, but rather on the electoral strategies representatives adopt in response to particular types of constituencies. Two conflicting hypotheses have been proposed.

In *Dimensions of Congressional Voting*, Duncan MacRae wrote:

Conceivably a representative of one major party may attain sufficient control over his district to become a spokesman not merely of "partisan" interests (e.g., labor, if he is a Democrat), but to some extent of the district as a whole. By taking a middle-of-the-road position on many matters, including his roll-call votes, he may be able to increase his security in the district.[56]

Similarly, in *An Economic Theory of Democracy* Anthony Downs argued that under certain conditions competing candidates would converge to the position of the median citizen in the electorate.[57] Downs also argued that divergence would occur under certain conditions, but later developments in spatial modeling have emphasized convergence even under conditions Downs considered sufficient to produce divergence.[58] Building on Downsian arguments Robert Erikson hypothesizes that

1. For a Republican Congressman: the more conservative he is, the more his vote margins will be reduced.
2. For a Democratic Congressman: the more liberal he is, the more his vote margin will be reduced.[59]

Thus, we have the hypothesis that in competitive situations representatives can increase their vote by taking moderate, middle-of-the-road positions. Conversely, policy extremity will lead to poorer showings at the polls. But by no means is there universal agreement about this argument. Samuel Huntington, for one, contends that the dynamics of competition in one-party districts produce "me-too" modal candidates, whereas competitive districts produce candidates with distinct positions aimed at different segments of the district.[60]

Turning to the data, we have seen that representatives from competitive districts typically desert their party on occasion to cast some votes with the opposition, while their safe counterparts maintain a solid partisan front. Thus, marginal representatives apparently tend toward middle-of-the road positions, whereas safe representatives opt for doctrinal purity. Erikson concludes that his arguments definitely hold for Republicans although the evidence is less clear for Democrats. On the other hand, Huntington presents data which he believes support his arguments. So, who is correct? Does electoral competition encourage convergence, divergence, neither, or both?[h]

---

[h]One should note that the arguments of Huntington and Erikson probably are not *logically* inconsistent, just empirically so. Huntington could be correct that electoral competition produces candidate divergence, and Erikson also correct, that divergence depresses vote margins. Such a state of affairs would call into question the Downsian model and subsequent extensions in that candidates would be failing to maximize their electoral chances even though an available course of action would enable them to do so.

Again, we believe that the conflict is more apparent than real, for a serious confusion runs through this research area. Briefly, an assertion that competition produces moderation (or extremism) contains much ambiguity, for, moderate and extreme are highly relative characterizations. Does one mean moderate (extreme) relative to one's fellow officials, or relative to one's constituents? Typically empirical studies analyze data concerning the first relationship and make an inferential leap about the second. Unfortunately, a representative's position in the legislative arena in principle reveals little about his position in the constituency arena, and vice versa. The remainder of this section elaborates on this "two-arenas" theme.

Consider first the "revised theory" of Samuel Huntington. Taking exception to the prevailing view that the qualitative difference (i.e., policy spread) between political parties varies *directly* with the quantitative difference (i.e., vote disparity), Huntington proposed a new theory: the qualitative difference between the parties varies *inversely* with the quantitative difference.

... in some areas there will be two similar but unequally balanced parties and in other areas two equally balanced but dissimilar parties. In terms of an interest group analysis this means of course that instead of appealing to all groups the parties will limit their appeal to certain specific groups. They will attempt to win elections by mobilizing a high degree of support from a small number of interests rather than by mustering a relatively low degree of support from a large number of interests.[61]

By and large, researchers on constituency influence have rejected the revised theory. This is unfortunate because, as we will demonstrate in Chapter 5, the revised theory predicts correctly. Why then has the theory met rejection? Simply because most researchers—Huntington included—misinterpret the revised theory.

Table 1-1 illustrates the data which Huntington presented as the principal test of his theory. At first glance the theory appears quite accurate. As the quantitative difference between the parties increases, the qualitative difference

Table 1-1
Test of Huntington's Revised Theory

Type of District	Average Republican Liberalism Index		Average Democratic Liberalism Index	Average N. Democratic Liberalism Index
Marginal	20.3	(69.6)	89.9	89.9
Close	20.4	(60.4)	80.8	84.5
Close intermediate	17.7	(58.3)	76.0	85.0
Solid intermediate	13.8	(50.0)	63.8	76.4
Solid	22.2	(22.5)	44.7	86.3

Source: Samuel Huntington, "A Revised Theory of American Party Politics," *American Political Science Review*, 44 (1950), p. 671.

(in parentheses) decreases (69.6 to 22.5). But as Shannon points out, Huntington's theory is confirmed more by virtue of historical accident than descriptive potency.[62] It happens to be the case that many safe Democratic districts are rural, agrarian Southern districts, while many safe Republican districts are rural, agrarian Mid-Western districts. But for historical factors Representatives from these districts might have found themselves in the same party; sometimes they do in the form of the so-called Conservative Coalition. If Southern Democrats are not considered, the qualitative difference between the parties is 69.6 in marginal districts and 64.1 in safe districts—not particularly supportive of Huntington's theory. Shannon goes on to present his own data which he interprets as inconsistent with Huntington's theory.[63] Lewis Froman comes to a similar conclusion.[64] Thus, in view of Shannon's criticism of Huntington's test and the additional conflicting evidence, one might think that the revised theory should be discarded. The evidence, however, deserves a closer look.

A careful reading of Huntington's article reveals that the data thus far brought to bear on the revised theory (including Huntington's) are irrelevant to the truth or falsity of its central proposition. Why? Because Huntington's theory predicts party differences *within* constituencies, not *between* constituencies. Huntington's arguments imply that *within* a competitive Congressional district the parties will be relatively further apart than they will *within* a given safe district. Thus, the proper test of the revised theory would be to examine the policy differences *between Congressmen and their opponents in marginal districts* and compare these with the differences *between Congressmen and their opponents in safe districts.* Interestingly, one critic of Huntington considers this point but summarily rejects it. Stone writes:

That Democratic and Republican *candidates* from safe districts do not differ radically is an interesting, but by the procedures used here, not a researchable possibility. At any rate such a finding would not save the "two cultures" thesis.[65]

We could not disagree more.

When researchers compare the average policy difference between marginal Republican and Democratic *legislators* with that between safe Republican and Democratic *legislators*, they cannot say anything one way or the other about Huntington's thesis. Regrettably, legislative researchers tend to confuse two distinct policy arenas: that of the legislature and that of the constituency. For example, Erikson argues that representatives who stray far from the median *of their districts* will suffer at the polls. But he states his hypothesis in terms of absolute liberalism and conservatism, and measures these *relative to other representatives.* Conceivably, a Republican who looks rather conservative in the House could look rather pink to his district. Similarly, MacRae remarks that

Our data for Massachusetts do not reveal extremely sharp ideological divergences between the parties in "intermediate" districts; rather they show a tendency for the parties to approach one another more closely in those districts where there is a contest between parties.[66]

Actually, MacRae's data show nothing of the kind. His data show that *within the legislature* marginal Democrats and Republicans appear closer than do safe Democrats and Republicans. But the data say nothing at all about party distances *within marginal districts vis-à-vis* those *within safe districts.* A representative can be simultaneously a constituency extremist and a legislative moderate, just the opposite, or an extremist or moderate in both arenas. One should examine one's hypotheses carefully to determine the arena to which they refer. Otherwise one may very well answer a question that was not asked.[i]

In sum, Huntington's theory is untested as yet. As we will show, some evidence in the literature does support the revised theory, as do data gathered to evaluate our own theoretical propositions. We present this evidence in Chapter 5. Since Huntington himself performed the first misconceived test of his theory, one cannot blame his critics for rejecting it. They criticize correctly Huntington's test, but not his theory.

What Is to be Done?

In this chapter we have attempted to isolate what we actually know about constituency influence on representatives' voting behavior. Our overall conclusion is that we tend to think we know more than we do. One class of studies illustrates the existence of constituency influence, though some have tried to infer more from these works. A second class of studies showers us with statistical relationships but justifies only one general conclusion: some constituency characteristics are weakly to moderately related to voting on some issue dimensions at some times. Other studies inform us that Congressmen vastly overestimate their impact on the voting of their constituents, and to a considerable extent vote as constituents desire, at least those Congressmen from safe districts. Finally, some studies suggest that representatives head for the middle-ground of their districts, but another study denies this conclusion. And existing data are irrelevant for both assertions.

The time to address another question now has arrived: given the state of the

---

[i]So far as we are able to ascertain, of those who have examined the link between party competition and policy moderation, only Miller is conscious of the distinction drawn in the text. In his article Miller presents data (Table 10-1, p. 295) that show that within the *Congress,* marginal Republicans and Democrats are closer in average roll-call position than are safe Republicans and Democrats in all three issue areas. But immediately thereafter (Table 10-3, p. 297) Miller shows that the candidates in marginal *districts* are much further apart in average SW policy attitudes than are the candidates in safe *districts.* Still, one should remember that Miller's intradistrict comparisons are based on policy attitudes. Although Miller characterizes attitudes as "first cousins to the roll-call records" (p. 296), his own data raise serious questions about the correspondence.

problem, where do we go next? Generally, there is something of a pat answer to questions of this type. One suggests that we need much more data, better measures, bigger and better statistical packages, and so forth. But perhaps the usual answer is not the complete answer.

Research findings are answers, answers to questions posed by researchers. If these answers are contradictory, vague, confused, highly conditional, or otherwise unsatisfactory, it is possible that our methods for answering the research questions are unsatisfactory. But it may be the case also, or instead, that the questions themselves are vague, confused or otherwise unsatisfactory.[j] If we don't know what we're looking for, quite likely we won't find it. Could the latter be the case in the constituency influence studies?

Consider the critical reaction to a hypothetical biologist who presents a paper on the relationship between oxygen and life. He reports that there is a positive correlation between the two, but that the relationship varies among forms of life, with amounts and purity of oxygen, and over time. He concludes that stable generalizations in this area are unlikely. We would not take such a character seriously. But look closely at our own work. When we ask whether there exists a relationship between two such amorphous variables as constituents' attitudes and legislators' aggregate votes, are we not in the position of the hypothetical biologist? We should hardly expect our answer to be a mathematical relationship invariant in time.

Too often it seems that the increasing availability of electronic computing facilities, data banks, and canned statistical packages has encouraged a concomitant decline in the use of our own capabilities. Rather than hypothesize we factor analyze, regress, and causal model. We speak of empirical theory as if it miraculously grows out of a cumulation of empirical findings, rather than as a logical structure one must carefully construct to explain those findings.

Without theory to guide our research we are unlikely to know precisely what we seek. One researcher tells us that he wishes to " . . . investigate the links between party and constituency characteristics and roll call votes."[6 7] Fine. But what links? Why should we expect to find any? In all states? On all issues? For all representatives? It is just such efforts which have led to the confusion about the "links between . . . constituency characteristics and roll-call votes." All too seldom do researchers tell us precisely what they expect to find and present a clear argument for why they expect to find it. For the most part we get only a summary of statistical associations along with some a posteriori rationalizations of these associations.

Now comes the hard part. To criticize is easy and enjoyable. To contribute to the professional literature is far more difficult, though even more enjoyable. In

---

[j]A third possibility—voiced distressingly frequently—is that political reality is "too complex." We are told that political behavior is subject to so many variable influences that large portions of it will remain forever inexplicable. This suggestion constitutes an end to research rather than an alternative such as refining questions or methods. Medical researchers are not paid to discover that illnesses are terminal. Political scientists might perhaps take a hint.

the remainder of this book we will give others something to criticize. The next three chapters contain a theoretical consideration of the relationship between constituents' preferences and representatives' voting. This theoretical analysis suggests an explanation for some findings already considered as well as others which we introduce where appropriate. Additionally, it implies a number of unexpected propositions, some of which may be tested with available data. Finally, we hope that the analysis will provide some guidance to future empirical investigations of constituency influence. That is, testing theories requires empirical studies. But theoretical guidance will make precision in study design and focus easier to attain. We will know what we are looking for before we go looking.

Notes

1. A good survey of this long controversy is provided in Hanna Pitkin (ed.), *Representation* (New York: Atherton Press, 1969). See also Heinz Eulau, "Changing Views of Representation," in Ithiel de Sola Pool (ed.), *Contemporary Political Science* (New York: McGraw-Hill, 1967), pp. 53-85.

2. For a survey of these ideas see Austin Ranney, *The Doctrine of Responsible Party Government* (Urbana: University of Illinois Press, 1954).

3. As the English seem to realize. Consider Brian Barry's *Sociologists, Economists and Democracy* (London: Collier-MacMillan, 1970).

4. Julius Turner, *Party and Constituency: Pressures on Congress* (Johns Hopkins Press, 1951). This work has been revised and updated. See Julius Turner and Edward Schneier, *Party and Constituency: Pressures on Congress* (Baltimore: Johns Hopkins Press, rev. ed., 1970).

5. Wayne Shannon, *Party Constituency and Congressional Voting* (Baton Rouge: Louisiana State University Press, 1968), p. 115 and the whole of Chapter 6.

6. Lewis Froman, "Inter-Party Constituency Differences and Congressional Voting Behavior," *American Political Science Review*, 57 (1963), 57-61.

7. On the question of personal political beliefs, see Lewis Froman, "The Importance of Individuality in Voting in Congress," *Journal of Politics*, 25 (1963), 324-332. Lee Anderson, "Individuality in Voting in Congress: A Research Note," *Midwest Journal of Political Science*, 8 (1964), 425-429.

8. Turner and Schneier, p. 114.

9. Duncan MacRae, "The Relation between Roll-Call Votes and Constituencies in the Massachusetts House of Representatives," *American Political Science Review*, 46 (1952), 1046-1055.

10. Ibid., p. 1055.

11. Thomas Dye, "A Comparison of Constituency Influences in the Upper and Lower Chambers of a State Legislature," *Western Political Quarterly*, 14 (1961), 473-481.

12. Hugh LeBlanc, "Voting in State Senates: Party and Constituency Influences," *Midwest Journal of Political Science*, 13 (1969), 33-57.

13. Samuel Patterson, "The Role of the Deviant in the State Legislative System: The Wisconsin Assembly," *Western Political Quarterly*, 14 (1961), 460-473.

14. Samuel Patterson, "Dimensions of Voting Behavior in a One-Party State Legislature," *Public Opinion Quarterly*, 26 (1962), 185-201.

15. Thomas Flinn, "Party Responsibility in the States: Some Causal Factors," *American Political Science Review*, 58 (1964), 60-71.

16. Ibid., pp. 70-71.

17. Pertti Pesonen, "Close and Safe State Elections in Massachusetts," *Midwest Journal of Political Science*, 7 (1963), 54-70.

18. Malcolm Parsons, "Quasi-Partisan Conflict in a One-Party Legislative System: The Florida Senate, 1947-1961," *American Political Science Review*, (1962), 605-614.

19. Wilder Crane and Meredith Watts, *State Legislative Systems* (Englewood Cliffs, New Jersey: Prentice-Hall, 1968), p. 87.

20. Lewis Froman, *Congressmen and their Constituencies* (Chicago: Rand McNally, 1963), pp. 94-95.

21. Ibid., p. 93.

22. Shannon, p. 154.

23. Ibid., pp. 159-161.

24. Ibid., pp. 161-163.

25. Froman, *Congressmen and their Constituencies*, p. 115.

26. Warren Miller, "Majority Rule and the Representative System of Government," in E. Allardt and Stein Rokkan (eds.), *Mass Politics* (New York: Free Press, 1970), pp. 284-311.

27. Ibid., p. 298, p. 304, p. 310, respectively.

28. Patterson, "The Role of the Deviant," p. 468.

29. "The Political Setting," in Alexander Heard (ed.), *State Legislatures in American Politics* (Englewood Cliffs: Prentice-Hall, 1966), p. 91.

30. *Party Loyalty Among Congressmen* (Cambridge: Harvard University Press, 1966), p. 23.

31. For discussion of these techniques see Lee Anderson, Meredith Watts, Jr., and Allen Wilcox, *Legislative Roll Call Analysis* (Evanston: Northwestern University Press, 1966). Duncan MacRae, Jr., *Issues and Parties in Legislative Voting* (New York: Harper and Row, 1970).

32. Duncan MacRae, Jr., *Dimensions of Congressional Voting* (Berkeley: The University of California Press, 1958).

33. N.L. Gage and B. Shimberg, "Measuring Senatorial Progressivism," *Journal of Abnormal and Social Psychology*, 44 (1949), 112-117.

34. Shannon, p. 155. More than anyone, Shannon emphasizes the time-bound character of generalizations about Congressional voting behavior.

35. Ibid., p. 151.

36. MacRae, *Dimensions*, p. 286.

37. Jack Van Der Slik, "Roll Call Voting in the House of Representatives of the 88th Congress: Constituency Characteristics and Party Affiliation," (Carbondale, Illinois: Public Affairs Research Bureau, Southern Illinois University, 1969).

38. Aage Clausen, *How Congressmen Decide: A Policy Focus* (New York: St. Martin's, 1973).

39. Ibid., p. 126, p. 128.

40. Ibid., pp. 136-137.

41. Ibid., p. 138.

42. Ibid., p. 139.

43. Ibid., Chapter 7.

44. Ibid., Chapter 7. See also Aage Clausen, "State Party Influence on Congressional Policy Decisions," *Midwest Journal of Political Science*, 16 (1972), 77-101.

45. John Jackson, "Some Indirect Evidences of Constituency Pressures on Senators," *Public Policy*, 16 (1967), 253-270.

46. John Jackson, "Statistical Models of Senate Roll Call Voting," *American Political Science Review*, 65 (1971), 451-470.

47. Thomas Flinn and Harold Wolman, "Constituency and Roll Call Voting: The Case of Southern Democratic Congressmen," *Midwest Journal of Political Science*, 10 (1966), 192-199.

48. John Kessel, "The Washington Congressional Delegation," *Midwest Journal of Political Science*, 8 (1964), 1-21.

49. Wilder Crane, "Do Representatives Represent?," *Journal of Politics*, 22 (1960), 295-299.

50. Shannon, pp. ix-x.

51. Warren Miller and Donald Stokes, "Constituency Influence in Congress," in R. Peabody and N. Polsby (eds.), *New Perspectives on the House of Representatives* (Chicago: Rand McNally, 2nd ed., 1969), pp. 33-34.

52. Ibid., pp. 31-54.

53. Donald Stokes and Warren Miller, "Party Government and the Saliency of Congress," *Public Opinion Quarterly*, 26 (1962), 531-546.

54. Ibid., p. 542.

55. Miller and Stokes, p. 48.

56. MacRae, *Dimensions*, p. 282.

57. Anthony Downs, *An Economic Theory of Democracy* (New York: Harper and Row, 1957), Chapter 8.

58. See, for example, Peter Ordeshook, "Extensions to a Model of the Electoral Process and Implications for the Theory of Responsible Parties," *Midwest Journal of Political Science*, 14 (1970), 43-70. Richard D. McKelvey, "Policy Related Voting and its Effects on Electoral Equilibrium: A Reformula-

tion and Generalization of Some Theorems on Abstention in Spatial Models of Party Competition," American Political Science Association Convention Paper, Washington, 1972. Richard McKelvey and Jeff Richelson, "Cycles of Risk," Public Choice Society Paper, College Park, Maryland, 1973.

59. "The Electoral Impact of Congressional Roll Call Voting," *American Political Science Review*, 65 (1971), 1018-1032.

60. Samuel Huntington, "A Revised Theory of American Party Politics," *American Political Science Review*, 44 (1950), 669-677.

61. Huntington, p. 675.

62. Shannon, pp. 166-170.

63. Ibid., p. 167.

64. Froman, *Congressmen and their Contituencies*, pp. 116-117.

65. Clarence N. Stone, "Issue Cleavage Between Democrats and Republicans in the U.S. House of Representatives," *Journal of Public Law*, 14 (1965), Footnote 34.

66. MacRae, "The Relation Between Roll Call Votes and Constituencies," p. 1054.

67. LeBlanc, p. 34.

2

Foundations of a Theory of Constituency Influence

Introduction

This chapter contains a presentation and discussion of the components of our theory. We will introduce and attempt to justify a number of concepts and assumptions which in combination make possible the analysis in later chapters. Like all theoretical worlds, the one we posit is more or less unrealistic, an idealization of the empirical reality we hope to explain. But if we abstract appropriately and capture the most important features of the empirical situation, then we may expect to find that the theoretical processes present in the model world bear some correspondence to the behavior we observe in the empirical world.

Parameters of the Voting Decision

Most fundamentally, we begin with the assumption that the representative is a purposive actor. His votes are not simply passive responses to role expectations, group memberships, and interest group pressures. Rather, the representative votes with an eye toward achieving valued consequences. As Mathews and Stimson argue,

> ... congressmen *attempt* to cast their votes so as to enhance the chances of achieving their goals. ... The potential payoffs to congressmen for casting roll-call votes in a reasonably rational way are so great and the potential risks of following any other course so large, that the members *try*, and *try hard*, to be reasonable.[1]

We do not believe that the assumption of goal-directed voting is particularly radical, although many investigators tend to view legislative voting more in deterministic than in purposive terms. The ultimate justification for the assumption, of course, is the explanatory power of theories based on it.

Given mass constituency unawareness of legislative issues and records, representatives apparently make their voting decisions in an atmosphere of great uncertainty about the political impact of those decisions. We assume that representatives deal with that uncertainty by making subjective judgments about the consequences of their votes and about other parameters of their decision situations. These subjective estimates then are processed as inputs into the voting decision problem. Thus, the representative's perceptions become the link between his constituents and his vote. More exactly, Bayesian decision theory provides the model for our substantive theory.[2] Bayesian theory purports to prescribe optimal decision making under uncertainty. Possibly, then, it is relevant to the voting decisions of representatives. A conceptual interpretation of the formal representation of a decision problem constitutes the theoretical structure that we use in formulating a theory of constituency influence.

In Table 2-1 the θ_j symbolize mutually exclusive and collectively exhaustive "states of nature," each of which has a probability, p_j ($0 \leqslant p_j \leqslant 1$, $\Sigma p_j = 1$) of occurrence. The a_i signify actions or strategies. An act, a_i, chosen when a state of nature, θ_j, holds results in a consequence, x_{ij} (which may be a set of specific outcomes). Decision theory addresses the question of the optimum choice of acts.[a]

To render this abstract representation empirically useful one must provide substantive interpretations of each of the formal concepts. What *states of nature* does the representative have in mind when he makes his voting decision? What *actions* or *strategies* are available to him? What *consequences* are perceived given the available strategies and the relevant states of nature? What does one mean by an *optimal strategy*? Answers to each of these questions depend to a great degree on the answer to a final one: what are the representative's *goals*?

To begin to answer the preceding questions consider the representative's *goals*

Table 2-1
Formal Decision Problem

Acts	States of Nature		
	$\theta_1 \ldots\ldots\ldots \theta_j \ldots\ldots\ldots \theta_n$		
a_1	$x_{11} \ldots\ldots\ldots x_{1j} \ldots\ldots\ldots x_{1n}$		
.	$\ldots\ldots\ldots\ldots\ldots\ldots\ldots\ldots\ldots$		
.	$\ldots\ldots\ldots\ldots\ldots\ldots\ldots\ldots\ldots$		
a_i	$x_{i1} \ldots\ldots\ldots x_{ij} \ldots\ldots\ldots x_{in}$		
.	$\ldots\ldots\ldots\ldots\ldots\ldots\ldots\ldots\ldots$		
.	$\ldots\ldots\ldots\ldots\ldots\ldots\ldots\ldots\ldots$		
a_m	$x_{m1} \ldots\ldots\ldots x_{mj} \ldots\ldots\ldots x_{mn}$		

[a]Bayesian decision theory differs from other decision theories in its conception of probability. For Bayesians, probability is not an objective measure (e.g., relative frequency) nor a logical relation between propositions (e.g., necessary probability). Rather, probability is a personal "degree of belief," a subjective judgment about the likelihood of occurrence of an event. For an explication of the Bayesian viewpoint, one should consult Leonard Savage, *The Foundations of Statistics* (New York: Wiley, 1954). The classic articles on the topic of subjective probability are available now in Henry E. Kyburg, Jr. and Howard E. Smokler (eds.), *Studies in Subjective Probability* (New York: Wiley, 1964).

in a general way. Empirically goals are numerous. Reelection, legislative influence, prestige, policy, higher office, public service—all may play their part.[3] But we would argue that reelection is the primary goal that the constituency controls: the district gives and the district can take away. Sometimes observers assume that representatives are not (or at least should not be) motivated by self-interest. Buchanan and Tullock comment wryly that we expect men to shift moral gears between the economic and political arenas.[4] Realistically or cynically as the case may be, we believe that constituents' preferences are reflected in a representative's voting (if at all) primarily through his concern for his electoral survival. Assume that each representative evaluates his situation by a subjective estimate, p, of his current probability of reelection.[b] That is, if the legislature were to adjourn today for the campaign, p would symbolize the representative's subjective probability of winning the election. We elaborate further on this estimate shortly.

It seems self-evident that the relevant *states of nature* involve the configuration of interested voters. Who cares, and on which side of the issue? The major difficulty with this suggestion is provided by the survey researchers' retort that "almost no one cares, ever." Thus, conceptualizing the states of nature poses the most difficult problem in formulating the theory.

We will assume, first, that the representative does not perceive his district as a collection of atomized voters who respond individually to his actions. Rather, we assume that the representative perceives his district as a collection of groups of voters with the members of each group holding like preferences. We use the term "group" as a kind of shorthand for the opinion sectors into which the representative divides the district; no false personification is implied. A group may be a well-defined formal entity such as COPE or the Possum Hollow Rod and Gun Club, a demographic segment of the constituency such as Catholics or blacks, or an "issue public" such as proprayer-in-schools. But in any case, the representative expects constituents to react to issues as members of a group; i.e., in their roles as union members or hunters or blacks rather than individual constituents.[c]

Second, we assume that the states of nature for the representative's decision are based on the judgments of groups of constituents that the issue at hand is relevant or irrelevant to their interests. Thus, if a representative believes his district contains two groups, G_1 and G_2, which might be interested in an issue,

---

[b]One should remember that probability of reelection is not equivalent to expected proportion of the vote, although the two should be related. It is perfectly possible for a representative who expects 55 percent of the vote to be more certain of reelection than one who expects 60 percent. The variance of the distribution of expected proportion of the vote is larger in the second case.

[c]We will be assuming that on each vote the contending groups are mutually exclusive. Such an assumption clearly would be ridiculous if applied to all votes, but we think it not unwarranted for single votes. On most votes alignments will be relatively nonoverlapping; e.g., business-labor, urban-rural, Republicans-Democrats, black-white, Catholic-Protestant.

then the states of nature are four: both G_1 and G_2 care about the issue; G_1 cares but not G_2; G_2 cares but not G_1; neither G_1 nor G_2 cares. Still, isn't the last state the case for all but the most well-organized groups? Is the problem of constituent apathy still with us, but at the group rather than the individual level? Our answer involves a special interpretation for the concept of "care."

Even though numerous informed constituents seldom pressure the representative directly, one suspects that the following question frequently crosses his mind: "What is the likelihood that this vote will provide a campaign issue that will activate the members of G_j?"[d] We take the answer to this question, c_j, as an estimate of the probability that G_j cares. Thus, *we conceptualize caring not as the actual state of concern of constituents at the time of the vote, but rather as their receptivity when the vote is brought to their attention during a future campaign.*[e] Thus, the somewhat elusive probability that a group, G_j, cares about an issue, k, reflects the somewhat harder probability estimate, c_{jk}, that the representative's vote on issue k will provide a campaign issue which will move the members of G_j during the next election campaign. In effect, the probability that a group cares is not a current measurement. Rather, it is a judgment about a future state that exists after a representative and his opponent(s) have made their efforts to inform groups of the record.

Expressions of the preceding argument are not at all uncommon in the literature. For example, Clausen writes humorously but insightfully,

my image of the constituency is that of a somnolent giant usually oblivious to the representative's existence. However, this giant has certain tender spots that must be protected from the prodding opponent who would like to arouse the giant and turn its wrath on the negligent representative. To guard against this eventuality, the representative must constantly reexamine the otherwise placid constituency to locate the tender spots and provide the needed protection against the pesky opponent.[5]

And Gregory notes that

... it is ... arguable that it is a characteristic of the politician to see the chance of penalties and rewards where others see only public indifference and ignorance.[6]

Clearly, arguments like these rely on Carl Friedrich's "law of anticipated reactions."[7] If this mechanism fails, then in all likelihood, so will our theory.

In sum, survey findings about voter apathy and ignorance do not invalidate our analysis. One should remember that reality is funneled through the

---

[d]As one of Clapp's interviewees commented, "When you measure pressure you measure it in terms of what the groups do *in an election period*" (my emphasis). Charles Clapp, *The Congressman: His Job as He Sees It* (Washington: Brookings, 1963), p. 187.

[e]Again, "You must be as smart in prospect as they [the voters] are in retrospect." Ibid., p. 178.

representative's perceptions, a point Dexter emphasized more than twenty years ago.[8] *Less important than whether constituents actually care is whether the representative thinks they can be made to care.*

The *actions* open to a representative are to vote for or against a bill. Simultaneously the vote signals adoption of a position for and/or against groups of constituents who care about the issue, unless all are estimated to be totally indifferent. Thus, if a representative estimates that groups 1 and 2 favor a bill and groups 3 and 4 oppose it, we characterize his voting strategies as a_1: vote with G_1 and G_2; and a_2: vote against G_1 and G_2. In Chapter 4 we admit a third strategy, abstention, and analyze its effects.

Let each representative measure the *consequences* of his actions in terms of increments, x, and decrements z, in his subjective probability, p, of reelection. That is, given that a group cares, the representative estimates that voting with the group results in some increase (at least no loss) in support from the group. Thus, his subjective probability of reelection rises from p to $(p + x)$, where $x \geqslant 0$. Conversely, if the representative votes against the group, he expects some loss (at least no gain) in support from the group. This reduced support is reflected in a lower probability of reelection $(p - z)$, where $z \geqslant 0$. Define the *strength*, S_{jk}, of a group, G_j, with respect to an issue, k, as $(x_{jk} + z_{jk})$. That is, a representative judges a group's strength on an issue according to their estimated total capability, $(x_{jk} + z_{jk})$, of changing his subjective probability of reelection. Henceforth, when we speak of stronger and weaker groups we use the term in this specific sense. Only groups for whom the representative estimates a nonzero strength need be considered in the decision calculus. Such groups we term *significant*. But notice that the representative determines significance, not the researcher.

In sociological terms the x_{jk}, z_{jk} are perceived positive and negative sanctions, respectively. Those who study sanctions have distinguished two components, a power or capability component, and an effectiveness or credibility component.[9] To expand somewhat, a group has a certain sanctioning capability, if exercised, but also a certain likelihood of delivering. We have attempted to capture these components in the x_{jk}, z_{jk}, and c_{jk}, respectively. The x_{jk} and z_{jk} are to be interpreted as the aggregate payoffs if the group should react to a campaign issue stemming from the representative's vote. The c_{jk} represents the estimate that the vote does become an issue. We assume that the x_{jk} and z_{jk} estimates are independent of the c_{jk} estimate. That is, the representative is capable of separating the power or capability component from the likelihood component. Empirically, decision makers sometimes tend to confound their evaluations of payoffs with the probabilities of attaining them.[10] Theoretically, though, we require greater exactitude from the political decision makers.

A final comment—our analysis takes the strength estimates as given. Clearly, these aggregate estimates must be functions of numerous arguments. The latter would include a group's size, its control of resources such as money, media and workers, its properties as a reference group for other constituents, etc. Ideally, one would like a theory of how representatives combine such diverse elements into an overall strength estimate. That is a topic for future research. For the present we simply assume that representatives somehow manage to make such estimates.[f]

All of the concepts introduced combine to make up the schematic voting-decision problem. Table 2-2 illustrates the interpreted decision problem for a very simple case: the representative's district is homogeneous with respect to the issue at hand (e.g., the 1957 Civil Rights Act in a Mississippi black belt district).

Several additional comments now are in order. First, we require that $x \leq (1 - p)$. If not, $(p + x)$, the representative's subjective probability of reelection after a vote "with" his constituents, may be greater than one. Similarly, $z \leq p$ insures that $(p - z)$ following an "against" vote will not be negative. Decision theorists have demonstrated that if decision makers are coherent, their subjective probability estimates will obey all the properties of the usual probability calculus.[g] We impose such a consistency requirement on the model representatives. Second, if $c = 0$, the decision problem evaporates: both voting strategies yield equivalent results. For this reason, the analysis considers only nondegenerate decision problems—those for which $c_j > 0$ for at least one significant G_j. Thus, we do not attempt to predict every representative's vote on every issue. If a representative estimates that $c_j = 0$, $\forall_j$, on a vote, that vote is outside the scope of the theory.

Table 2-2
Interpreted Decision Problem

Vote	State Probability	Constituency (i.e., Whites)	
		Cares (c)	~ Care $(1 - c)$
With		x	0
Against		$-z$	0
			where $x \leq (1 - p)$
			$z \leq p$

---

[f]For additional remarks on the conceptualization of the c_{jk}, x_{jk}, and z_{jk}, see Chapter 4.
[g]"Coherence" is a technical term used by Bayesians. Essentially, if one's subjective judgments are coherent, it is impossible to formulate a series of bets such that one is sure to lose money. That possibility exists if one is incoherent. A necessary and sufficient condition for coherence is simply that the sum of the probabilities of n mutually exclusive and collectively exhaustive events is unity. See Bruno de Finetti, "Foresight: Its Logical Laws, Its Subjective Sources," in Kyburg and Smokler, pp. 93-158.

Motivational Assumptions

Although we have specified a representative's primary goal as reelection, as yet we have presented no precise criteria by which to identify an *optimal strategy*. In decision theory one assumes ordinarily that the decision maker is a maximizer. He always prefers more of a positively valued consequence to less of it, or less of a negatively valued consequence to more of it. If one were to assume that the representative's goal was to maximize his subjective probability of reelection, one would define an optimal strategy as one which maximizes his expected subjective probability increment. Referring to Table 2-2, a representative would choose to vote "with" on all decisions taking this form.

Maximizing assumptions have a long and honorable tradition. Of course, such assumptions are idealizations, but they appear to be sufficiently good approximations that useful theories can be based on them. Still, legislative researchers know that besides reelection, numerous other goals—legislative influence, policy, prestige, party loyalty, higher office—are quite important to many legislators. Can one ignore such goals? By no means, in our opinion. But, let us examine the question of goals more closely.

An important fact to remember is that there is no necessary incompatibility between a desire to maximize electoral support and a desire to achieve other ends. Many legislators may find that the various things they desire can be attained by the same behavior. For example, consider a John McCormack. Certainly, there is little reason to believe that maximizing support in his Irish working-class district would conflict with his New Deal Policy beliefs and his partisan leadership position. Those representatives whose goals are mutually reinforcing might as well maximize electoral support, for by doing so they simultaneously accomplish other ends. Thus, for representatives whose goals are congruent, to assume that they aspire to electoral certainty may be an oversimplification, but not a serious one.

Still, there are Frank Smiths in the world as well as John McCormacks:[11] That is, some representatives find their electoral goals not always consistent with other things they value—policies they favor, and legislative party loyalties in particular. Depending on the importance of these other goals relative to electoral support, the assumption of maximizing probability of reelection may be unacceptably inaccurate for such representatives. Were we willing to postulate utility functions defined over broadly specified packages of consequences, no problem would arise. A greater utility necessarily represents a more preferred set of outcomes than a lesser utility. But the introduction of utility functions invariably introduces severe difficulties in applying the theory. Rather than trade empirical applicability for theoretical generality, we have attempted to approach the matter of motivation another way. This alternative path utilizes ideas reminiscent of both lexicographic preference structures and man-as-satisficer.

As stated previously, let us assume that reelection is a representative's primary goal. One need not adopt a highly cynical view of politics to take such a position; rather one need only recognize that without achieving the office, the benefits of office are unattainable. Defeat means the loss of the opportunity to shape public policies, the loss of the opportunity to wield power, and the loss of future opportunities to help one's legislative party. Thus, reelection is naturally a representative's primary consideration; everything else naturally takes second place.[h] But certainly there is no need to postulate that reelection is the *only* consideration.

Instead, following a well-known argument of Herbert Simon, let us assume that every representative establishes an aspiration level for his probability of reelection.[12] This level signifies a "satisfactory" probability of retaining office. Until they attain their aspiration levels, representatives can be expected to follow maximizing strategies. Additionally, representatives who set extremely high aspiration levels may resemble maximizers. But some representatives may set their aspiration levels low enough that they bear a significant amount of electoral risk. Once a representative's probability of reelection equals or surpasses his aspiration level he may direct some attention elsewhere. He ceases maximizing efforts and shifts to a maintaining effort.

To translate the preceding heuristic argument into a precise formal statement requires more if's, and's, and but's than we would like. But we have little to go on. Numerous researchers have argued about satisficing behavior in an informal manner, but there is a paucity of attempts to formalize such arguments.[13] Assume that first and foremost, representatives attempt to keep p within an internal, $[p^*, 1]$, $0 \leqslant p^* \leqslant 1$, where p^* denotes an aspiration level, a minimum acceptable subjective probability of reelection. So long as $p < p^*$, a representative attempts to maximize p: attainment of any goals other than an increased probability of reelection depends entirely on whether actions to attain them coincide with pursuit of the reelection goal. When $p^* \leqslant p \leqslant 1$, however, the representative ceases the maximizing effort and contents himself with doing no worse than breaking even in his voting. Define a *maintaining strategy* as one which assigns weights $(Q, 1 - Q)$, $0 \leqslant Q \leqslant 1$, to a_1 and a_2 in such a way as to result in no expected change in p. The set of *feasible strategies* for a maintainer, then is the continuum of two-tuples between $[Q, (1 - Q)]$ and $(1, 0)$, or $(0, 1)$ and $[Q, (1 - Q)]$, depending upon the decision. Any mixed strategy in this interval is acceptable in that it leads to no expected decline in p. The maintaining representative can choose whichever feasible strategy has associated

[h]In a lexicographic preference structure, a decision maker orders the dimensions of choice by their importance to him. He chooses the alternative whose expected outcome ranks highest on the first dimension, examining less important dimensions only in the event of ties on higher ones. The maintaining representative divides the dimensions of choice into two categories: probability of reelection, which is primary, and all others. He satisfices on the first dimension before looking to any other. This conceptualization is partially lexicographic, but certainly not completely so.

with it the most attractive package of secondary rewards. This latter strategy is his actual *optimal strategy*.

Clearly, then, a maintaining representative theoretically has more latitude in voting than a maximizing representative. The latter simply chooses the strategy with the highest expected reelection value. If all other goals conflict with this strategy, he foregoes them. The maintaining representative typically has a continuum of strategies from which to choose. He is restricted by a Q level which usually will be less than one. If all other goals conflict with the electoral goal, he still has a chance $(1 - Q)$ of attaining them. If all other goals are consonant with the electoral goal, he simply chooses the maximizing strategy. And, of course, everything in between is available to him. Notice that theoretical results about maximizing strategies translate into *exact* behavioral hypotheses. But theoretical results about maintaining strategies usually translate only into behavioral hypotheses which establish a *bound* on behavior. The maintaining strategy is not an exact prediction; it only sets a floor under a representative's voting; i.e., a representative must vote for a bill with probability *at least Q*. The assumption of maintaining behavior refers to the representative's desire at least to maintain a current position, not to a prediction that he votes so as to maintain p precisely unchanged. The latter prediction certainly would be wrong when other goals do not conflict with the electoral goal.

Two further points merit attention. First, because maintaining strategies typically are mixed, the optimal strategies eventually settled on by maintainers also may be mixed, particularly in cases of conflict among goals. While these mixed strategies yield no *expected* decline in p, on a single vote a representative might slip below his aspiration level. We will assume that such short-term stochastic falls in p below the level, p^* do not change the character of the representative from maintainer to maximizer. Over time, the laws of mathematical expectation will take care of the situation.

On the other hand, a more serious question may arise. Suppose a representative consistently chooses strategies which earn more constituency credit than the basic maintaining strategies. Eventually he then reaches a state where p is clearly higher than p^*. At such time the maintaining strategies calculated on the basis of no expected decline in p become too restrictive. For, seemingly the representative can afford to lose some probability of reelection. What does one predict about such a case? Here again we will follow Simon's discussion. Simon suggests that if decision makers find decisions "easy" in the sense that many alternatives produce outcomes all of which exceed the decision maker's aspiration level, a natural reaction of the decision maker is to up the level.[14] In this manner the range of originally satisfactory alternatives narrows to a subset of superior ones. Particularly in view of the assumed partially lexicographic preference structure of the representative, we believe such an assumption is appropriate here. If a representative's voting causes p to rise significantly above p^*, this would indicate that there is more consonance in the representative's goals than the original choice of p^* presumed. In effect, the original choice of p^* involves more electoral risk than the representative need bear. Thus, he can afford to raise p^*. We might expect p^* to "track" p, eventually reaching a kind of equilibrium level which denotes the greatest electoral security consistent with achieving conflicting secondary goals. Over time, optimal strategies converge to maintaining strategies as p^* varies.

Empirically, having the representative raise his aspiration level rather than drop his probability of reelection back to the old level appears reasonable to us. Opponents in the district may be encouraged by any sign that the representative's electoral position is deteriorating, regardless of his absolute position. Knowing this, a maintaining representative may not consciously strive to exceed his aspiration level, but once beyond it, he believes it imprudent to slip back.

To sum up the motivational discussion, the analysis to follow examines and compares the behavior of two types of representative. The first is the maximizer. A new representative might be working his way up to an initial aspiration level. A representative might have erred seriously on a vote, causing p to tumble far below p^*. A redistricting which removes old supporters or adds new opponents might affect p similarly. Those who desire subjective certainty ($p^* = 1$) can attain and maintain it only by behaving as maximizers, if then. And finally, those representatives who find a happy congruence among their goals can afford to maximize: their high aspiration level does not interfere with the attainment of secondary goals. For want of a better term we call the second type of representative the maintainer. He satisfies the condition $p^* \leqslant p \leqslant 1$. Having attained or exceeded his aspiration level he is content merely to avoid losing support. Any further gain is accidental. Thus, we have posited two ideal types of representative. Admittedly, both are approximations, as theoretical constructs always are. Hopefully two approximations will allow a more comprehensive analysis than one.

The Ungrateful Electorate

Only one task now remains before proceeding with the analysis. Optimal decision making involves a weighing of gains and losses. But thus far we have spoken of the costs and benefits to the hypothetical representative only in the most general terms. Indeed, all we have said is that a vote in accord with a group of constituents, G_j, merits an increment, x_j, while a vote against them incurs a decrement, z_j. We have specified no relationship between x_j and x_k, or z_j and z_k. Nor have we specified any relationship between x_j and z_j. The first set of relationships requires no special assumption. Without loss of generality, in each decision problem we will list the groups in order of their estimated strength. Thus, for a two-group decision, $(x_{1_k} + z_{1_k}) \geqslant (x_{2_k} + z_{2_k})$. In general, $S_{1_k} \geqslant S_{2_k} \geqslant \ldots \geqslant S_{n_k}$.

As for the relationship between x_{jk} and z_{jk}, we do impose an a priori restriction. Specifically, we assume that $z_{jk} \geqslant x_{jk}$, $\forall_j, \forall_k$. That is, given that a group cares about an issue, we assume that the representative believes that a vote in accord with the interest of the group gains him relatively less credit than a vote against their interest loses. This assumption expresses a rather common bit of political folklore. V.O. Key, Jr., once observed that perhaps voters vote "against," not "for."[15] Political scientists all will remember Alben Barkley's classic, "What have you done for me lately?" anecdote.[16] And in a splendid example of the sentiment we attempt to capture, a Tennessee voter observes

I think most people in Tennessee would like to vote Democratic because they make more money under the Democrats. But it's the people who're running as Democrats this time that make the difference. Voters aren't for Brock, they're against Gore. *And a man will stand in line at the polls a lot longer to vote against somebody than he will to vote for somebody.* (Our emphasis)[17]

Admittedly, the assumption that $z_{jk} \geqslant x_{jk}$, $\forall_j, \forall_k$ will violate reality on occasion. For example, if a representative believes $p = 0$ prior to a given vote, consistency requires that he estimate $z_j = 0$, $\forall_j$ on that vote. Yet in this situation seemingly x_j could be positive for some G_j. Another example, if a representative estimates that 100 percent of a group oppose him, he might reasonably believe that they can't hurt him any more, but that they could help. But although the assumption may be empirically wrong at times, the violations probably occur in extreme situations like the above. Most of empirical reality lies between the extremes, so we trust the assumption will lead to no serious error, and it may capture an important aspect of the representative's environment.

While the ordering of groups from those with greatest perceived electoral strength to those with least, and the assumption that $z_j \geqslant x_j$, the theoretical structure now contains enough detail to permit the deduction of various behavioral propositions. A compact summary of the substantive concepts and assumptions introduced and discussed in this chapter precedes the analysis.

Summary

Let p = the representative's subjective estimate of his current probability of reelection.

p^* = the representative's minimum "acceptable" subjective probability of reelection.

G_j = a significant group whom a representative estimates to be potentially concerned about an issue.

c_{jk} = the representative's subjective estimate that his vote on issue k will draw G_j into the next election campaign.

x_{jk} = the expected increment in p resulting from voting as the members of G_j prefer on issue k.

z_{jk} = the expected decrement in p resulting from not voting as the members of G_j prefer on issue k.

S_{jk} = the "strength" of G_j on issue k: $S_{jk} = (x_{jk} + z_{jk})$.

a_1 = a vote with a set of groups who take a position on an issue.

a_2 = a vote against the set of groups who prefer a_1 —by implication, a vote with a set of groups who hold an opposing preference.

Maximizer = a representative who votes with the sole intention of maximizing p.

Maintainer = a representative content to "break even" on each vote.

$[Q, (1-Q)]$ = a maintaining strategy.

Assumptions About Parameters of the Voting Decision

1. The states of nature are all the possible combinations in which n groups may "care" or not care;
2. The probabilities of the states of nature are calculated by combining the estimated c_{jk}'s, where the latter are assumed to be independently distributed:
3. The payoffs are the estimated x_{jk}'s and z_{jk}'s, where these are assumed to be independent of the c_{jk}'s.
4. $z_{jk} \geq x_{jk}$, $\forall_j$, $\forall_k$, where these numbers are constrained so as to satisfy the usual probability assumptions.

Motivational Assumption

A representative votes so as to raise his subjective probability of reelection, p, to a level, p^*, $(0 \leq p^* \leq 1)$.

1. Until p reaches the level p^* a representative votes so as to maximize p.
2. If p comes to exceed p^*, a representative raises p^*.

One final remark: we have constructed an almost completely subjective model. Thus, the p, G_j, c_j, and S_j need not correspond to the judgments or measurements of outside observers. We believe that the explanation for a representative's voting behavior lies in his perceptions, not in ours. We may console ourselves with the supposition that those representatives who grossly misjudge the empirical situation probably do not survive long in the electoral arena.[1] But while they do, their judgments, however distorted, explain their voting.

---

[1] Some evidence for this supposition appears in an article on Iowa legislators' perceptions of their constituents' opinions. The legislators were asked to judge whether each of four proposed constitutional amendments would receive majority backing in their districts in an upcoming referendum. Of those representatives with two or more incorrect predictions, 11

Notes

1. Donald Matthews and James Stimson, "Decision-Making by U.S. Representatives: A Preliminary Model," in S. Sydney Ulmer (ed.), *Political Decision-Making* (New York: Van Nostrand, 1970), pp. 16-17.

2. For a good introduction to Bayesian decision theory see Howard Raiffa, *Decision Analysis* (Reading, Massachusetts: Addison-Wesley, 1968); Robert Schlaifer, *Analysis of Decisions Under Uncertainty* (New York: McGraw-Hill, 1967).

3. For a discussion of Congressional goals, see Richard Fenno, *Congressmen in Committees* (Boston: Little Brown, 1973), Chapter 1.

4. James Buchanan and Gordon Tullock, *The Calculus of Consent* (Ann Arbor: University of Michigan Press, 1962), p. 210.

5. Clausen, *How Congressmen Decide.*

6. Roy Gregory, "Local Elections and the Rule of Anticipated Reactions," *Political Studies*, 57 (1969), p. 32. For similar arguments, see Roger Davidson, The Role of the Congressman (New York: Pegasus, 1969), p. 121. John Kingdon makes several of the same points in an argument on p. 154 of *Candidates for Office: Beliefs and Strategies* (New York: Random House, 1966).

7. Carl Friedrich, *Man and His Government* (New York: McGraw-Hill, 1963), pp. 199-215.

8. Lewis A. Dexter, "The Representative and his District," *Human Organization*, 16 (1947), 2-13.

9. See, for instance, Jerry B. Michel and Ronald C. Dillehay, "Reference Behavior Theory and the Elected Representative," *Western Political Quarterly*, 22 (1969), p. 771.

10. For evidence supporting both sides of the question, see F.W. Irwin, "Stated Expectations as Functions of Probability and Desirability of Outcomes," *Journal of Personality*, 21 (1953), 329-335. R. Duncan Luce and E.F. Shipley, "Preference Probability Between Gambles as a Step Function of Event Probability," *Journal of Experimental Psychology*, 63 (1962), 42-49.

11. Frank Smith, *Congressman from Mississippi* (New York: Pantheon, 1964).

12. Herbert Simon, *Models of Man* (New York: Wiley, 1957), Chapter 14.

13. Two papers which contain an informal discussion of satisficing vs. maximizing behavior among representatives are Donald Cell, "Maximizing,

of 59 were defeated. Of those with one or zero incorrect predictions, 11 of 122 were defeated. Those who badly misperceived constituency opinion had twice as high a rate of defeat as their more accurate colleagues. See Ronald Hedlund and H. Paul Friesema, "Representatives' Perceptions of Constituency Opinion," *Journal of Politics*, 34 (1972), p. 745. See also, David Segal and Thomas Smith, "Congressional Responsibility and the Organization of Constituency Attitudes," in Dan Nimmo and Charles Bonjean (eds.), *Political Attitudes and Public Opinion* (New York: David McKay Company, Inc., 1972), pp. 562-568.

Satisficing, and Discretionary Power," Public Choice Society Paper, Blacksburg, Va., 1971. David Koehler and Robert Oshel, "Electoral Margins and Legislative Voting Power: A Test of the Relationship between Electoral Strategies and Legislative Effectiveness," Public Choice Society Paper, College Park, Md., 1973.

14. Simon, p. 253.

15. V.O. Key, Jr., *The Responsible Electorate* (New York: Vintage, 1966), p. 60.

16. Alben Barkley, *That Reminds Me* (New York: Doubleday, 1954).

17. Richard Harris, "Annals of Politics: How the People Feel," *New Yorker*, July 10, 1971, p. 48.

3

A Simple Theory of Constituency Influence

Introduction

When combined, the set of ideas advanced in Chapter 2 constitute a highly simplified model of a representative's world as he ponders whether to cast a yea or nay. In this chapter we will ascertain how model representatives would behave in several of the contingencies which might arise in this model world. Three constituency configurations are examined. First, we will analyze the voting decision given a consensual or homogeneous district; i.e., a situation in which the groups who possibly care about the issue would agree on what the representative should do. Such homoegeneity seldom will hold across *all* issues in a real world district, but on particular issues it is probably often the case that only one group cares. Additionally, the fairly common "God, Motherhood, and Apple Pie" votes no doubt find all significant constituency groups in accord.

Our other two configurations involve the voting decision given a conflictual or heterogeneous district; i.e., a situation in which two significant constituency groups are in opposition. First, we will examine the voting decision when the issue is highly salient—sure to become a campaign issue. Then we turn to the more general case in which potential conflict exists, but the campaign impact is less certain.

To give the reader a better idea of where we are going, we suggest here that the analysis in this chapter provides a plausible model of the voting behavior of representatives from safe and marginal districts. That is, in the real world, districts which vote overwhelmingly for a representative are those which tend to be homogeneous in their structure of group interests. Conversely, districts which give representatives narrow margins are those which contain conflicting group interests. That electoral safety goes with district homogeneity and electoral marginality with district heterogeneity is by no means a new argument. In Chapter 5 we note the works of numerous political scientists who have made such an observation. Additionally, we present some data bearing on the correspondence. Interestingly, though, the analysis in this chapter helps to explain just *why* safety should accompany district homogeneity and marginality heterogeneity. We shall elaborate as the analysis proceeds.

Roll-Call Voting Decisions with a
Consensual Constituency

Consider the decision matrix given in Table 2-2 of the previous chapter: $c_j > 0$ for only one group in the constituency, or the entire constituency constitutes a single group for which $c_j > 0$. A representative never faces a less ambiguous situation. How does he behave?

For a maximizer, the answer is trivial. Voting with one's constituents is a dominant strategy: no matter what the state of nature, voting with one's constituents is at least as good and sometimes better than voting against them. This conclusion holds no matter what the strength of the group nor what the probability that they care. Thus, given a consensual district a maximizer is completely a slave to constituents' preferences. Empirically, then, if safe districts are those which tend to be homogeneous, and new representatives tend to be maximizers, one would expect that newly elected representatives from safe districts are maximally responsive to constituency wishes.

Now consider a maintaining representative. Recall that a maintainer regards an acceptable voting strategy as a discrete probability distribution over the strategy set such that the expected value of his vote, $E(\Delta p)$, exceeds or equals zero. Having attained his personal p^*, the maintainer is content to do no worse than break even on each vote. The exact maintaining strategy is easily calculated:

$$E(\Delta p) = 0 = Qcx + Q(1-c)0 + (1-Q)c(-z) + (1-Q)(1-c)0$$

$$= Qcx - xz + Qcz$$

$$cz = Qc(x+z)$$

$$\frac{z}{x+z} = Q \tag{3.1}$$

Equation (3.1) indicates the maintaining strategy for the homogeneous case. For example, if $z = .03$, $x = .02$, then $Q = .6$. Thus, a maintainer can vote with his constituents with any probability between .6 and 1.0 and still expect to satisfy the condition $p \geq p^*$. If his party leader is pushing him to vote against constituents, he can vote so as to maintain p exactly unchanged and still support the party leader with probability .4. Notice that $.5 \leq Q \leq 1$ because $z \geq x$, and $x + z > 0$.[a] A maintainer will end up voting with his constituents at least half the time on the average.

Several other features of Equation (3.1) deserve notice. First, Q increases or remains constant at its maximum as z increases: the greater the threat to a

[a]Recall that the representative includes in his decision problem only those G_j who (1) have nonzero c_j, and (2) are significant: $(x_j + z_j) = S_j > 0$.

representative's reelection that a constituency group can pose, the higher the probability that the representative must accede to their wishes. The proposition seems eminently plausible. Second, Q decreases as x increases: the greater the help to a representative's reelection that a constituency group can offer, the lower the probability that the representative must vote in accord with their wishes. This second proposition reflects the maintainer's intention only to maintain his probability of reelection. Within the framework of the theory, then, one finds a difference between the effects of gains and losses. So far as influencing a maintainer goes, potential losses are more important than potential gains. Constituents should threaten the stick, not promise the carrot. Notice finally that if $x = 0$, $Q = 1$ regardless of the value of z. In this case the maintaining strategy coincides with the maximizing strategy.

The $x = 0$ case has two seemingly plausible empirical interpretations. First, in some districts there exist "gut" issues for which constituents consider a vote with them as the very *sine qua non* of representation. A right vote merits no reward—any dutiful representative could only think of voting one way. Conversely, a wrong vote on such issues amounts to an abject betrayal of the representative's trust. These are the crucial issues on which constituency overrides all other considerations. As one example, we suggest Civil Rights votes in many Southern districts during the 1950s.[b] Abortion votes in some heavily Catholic districts provide another example.[c] On votes like these, homogeneous constituencies produce only maximizers.

A second interpretation involves not intense, "gut" issues, but rather "God, Motherhood, and Apple Pie" issues. Although opinion is homogeneous in such cases, it is likely that $x = 0$, since a representative hardly can expect to be rewarded for casting a vote in favor of Motherhood. Of course, a vote against Motherhood is another matter, so that $z > 0$.

---

[b]In their representation study Miller and Stokes relate the story of the defeat of Brooks Hays by Dale Alford in the Arkansas 5th District. Hays was perceived as a "moderate" on Civil Rights owing to his refusal to sign the Southern Manifesto, and to his service as an intermediary between Washington and Little Rock during the school crisis. More extreme than Hays, Alford won on a *write-in* vote! Moreover, *every* constituent interviewed had read or heard something about *both* candidates. The comparable national figure was 24 percent. See Miller and Stokes, "Constituency Influence in Congress," pp. 50-51.

[c]Consider the following case: In 1970 the "liberal" abortion bill passed by the New York Senate lay dead in the House apparently, 74 - 74 (a majority of the full membership of the House—76—is required to pass legislation). But before the Chair could announce the defeat of the bill, Representative George Michaels, a Democrat from a heavily Catholic district stepped to the microphone and changed his vote from "nay" to "aye." Speaker Perry Duryea then cast the 76th and winning vote. Michaels, previously best known for his bill naming the bluebird the state bird of New York, expressed the opinion that his vote switch was political suicide. Happily for believers in constituency influence, he was correct. Michaels was denied the nomination of the local party, defeated in the primary, and trounced in a three-way election. For those who might be interested, Michaels, a Jew, reported acting as he did from family pressures (one son called him a "political whore"). See the *New York Times*, Apr. 10, 1970, 1:8, 42:1, Apr. 20, 1970, 63:4; Apr. 23, 1970, 36:2; June 5, 1970, 40:4; Nov. 4, 1970, 19:1; Nov. 5, 1970, 43:3.

Another limiting case of empirical interest occurs in the event that a single group (or a unanimous district) has "make or break" power over a maintainer. That is, the group's support could render him certain of reelection, while their opposition could render him certain of defeat. In this case, the theoretical variables take on their maximum values. These are

$$z = p$$

$$x = z - \epsilon \quad \text{if } p \leqslant .5 \qquad\qquad \epsilon \geqslant 0$$

$$x = 1 - p \quad \text{if } p > .5$$

$$\text{If } p \leqslant .5, \ Q = \frac{p}{p - \epsilon + p} = \frac{p}{2p - \epsilon} \ \text{ and } \ \lim_{\epsilon \to 0} Q = \frac{1}{2}$$

$$\text{If } p > .5, \ Q = \frac{p}{1 - p + p} = p.$$

Thus, Q tends to ½ or to p *whichever is larger* in the case where a totally dominant constituency group exists. Interestingly, where one constituency group overshadows all others, the higher a maintainer's probability of reelection, the more bound to that group he becomes. A possible example of this phenomenon is the Southern Democratic Congressmen during much of the 1950s and 1960s. Because of constituency-legislative party conflict one might expect most of the Southern Democrats to be maintainers. On Civil Rights legislation their relevant constituency groups were blacks and whites, but owing to the disenfranchisement of the former, the effective constituency was homogeneous. Given that whites were a powerful enough group to make or break the Representative, one would expect that these Representatives showed a fealty to constituents which directly mirrored their own probability of reelection. The more confident they were, the more adamantly opposed to Civil Rights legislation they would have been. Although variation among the Southern Democrats on Civil Rights votes was slight, this hypothesis may be testable.

Leaving the question of payoffs aside for a moment, we call attention to a very interesting feature of Equation (3.1). In making his voting decision one might expect the representative to take into account the payoffs associated with each alternative and the probabilities of the states of nature. In our notation, $Q = f(c,x,z)$. But notice that one can write Equation (3.1) as $Q = f(x,z)$. That is, in the one group case the maintainer's choice of voting strategy does not depend on his estimate of the probability that the group cares. Whether $c = .01$ or $.99$ makes no difference. And, as previously mentioned, this conclusion applies as well to a maximizer's voting. Obviously, voting with the constituency group remains a dominant strategy no matter where in the internal $(0, 1.0)$ c falls.

Thus, *where an issue is of potential concern to only one group in a district, the actual probability they will respond to it is irrelevant to the representative's voting decision.*

Recall now the major reason for despairing of the existence of constituency influence: mass ignorance and apathy about legislative issues and records. But we have just found one theoretical situation in which mass unawareness of the representative's actions does not matter, so long as someone may be watching somewhere ($c > 0$). Thus, while the extent of voter awareness and information may be an interesting empirical question, a highly informed, issue-conscious constituency is *not* a necessary condition that must be met in order to link the representative's voting to his constituents' preferences.

Now let us turn to a slightly more complicated type of constituency homogeneity: two or more significant groups might be expected to care about the issue, but they would agree upon how the representative should vote.[d] Table 3-1 illustrates the voting decision problem for two significant groups.

Evidently, most of our previous conclusions do not change. For a maximizer, voting with the constituency groups is the dominant strategy, irrespective of the precise values of x, z, and c. For a maintainer, the maintaining strategy is given by Equation (3.2):

$$Q = \frac{c_1 z_1 + c_2 z_2}{c_1 x_1 + c_2 x_2 + c_1 z_1 + c_2 z_2} \tag{3.2}$$

Again, $Q \geqslant .5$ because $z_i \geqslant x_i$. And Q increases or does not change as either z_i increases, while Q decreases as either x_i increases. If $x_1 = x_2 = 0$, the maintaining strategy coincides with the maximizing strategy; i.e., $Q = 1$. These facts are exactly analogous to the one-group case and extend to any number of groups in the homogeneous case.

The one conclusion which changes concerns the relevance of the c_i for

Table 3-1
Voting Decision Given a Two-Group Consensual Constituency

Probability / State / Strategy	$G_1 G_2$ $c_1 c_2$	$G_1 \sim G_2$ $c_1 (1 - c_2)$	$\sim G_1 G_2$ $(1 - c_1) c_2$	$\sim G_1 \sim G_2$ $(1 - c_1)(1 - c_2)$
with	$x_1 + x_2$	x_1	x_2	0
against	$-z_1 - z_2$	$-z_1$	$-z_2$	0

[d]Perhaps real world representatives tend to combine all groups into two: pro and anti. If such were the case, the two-group consensual constituency would reduce to the one-group case just analyzed. Still, in the presence of significantly different c_j, keeping the multigroup structure of the problem intact seems advisable.

maintainer voting. Although the c_i again are irrelevant for maximizer voting, they are irrelevant for maintainer voting only in two special cases. First, if all the x_i equal zero, $Q = 1$ and does not vary as any of the c_i change. Second, if the c_i are equal, they are irrelevant to the maintainer's choice of strategy. Equality could arise either because of issue salience ($c_i = 1$, $\forall_i$), or because extreme uncertainty leads the representative to adopt a version of Laplace's Principle.[e]

Somewhat disappointingly, when the c_i are relevant to the voting decision, one cannot say exactly how they are relevant without additional conditions being imposed on the payoffs. One might suppose that as either c_i increases the probability a maintainer has to vote with his constituents similarly increases. Such is not the case. Q may increase, decrease or remain constant as the c_i vary. As constituted, the maintainer model yields no unique prediction about the relationship between Q and the c_i.

This completes our analysis of the consensual constituency. To recapitulate, the following set of conclusions follows from the analysis:

1. Maximizers always vote with constituents; maintainers do so at least half the time on the average.
2. In the one-group case, no representative votes any differently when his estimate that constituents care is high from when it is low.
3. In the multigroup case, maximizers still are not influenced by the probabilities that constituents care; maintainers are not influenced only if $x_i = 0, \forall_i$, or if $c_i = c_j, \forall_{i,j}$.
4. The voting flexibility of maintainers increases as the perceived positive sanctions of constituents increase, while flexibility decreases as perceived negative sanctions increase (unless $x_i = 0$, $\forall_i$, in which case maintaining requires maximizing which involves no flexibility).

Consider briefly now the implications of these conclusions for the voting behavior of representatives from safe districts. If safe districts tend to be homogeneous districts, one should not expect to find safe representatives free to ignore their constituents as some have suggested. Rather, these representatives will vote with constituents at least half the time on average. Indeed, the analysis suggests the major reason consensual districts tend to be safe districts. In such districts there exists a maximizing strategy which leads *at worst* to no loss in subjective probability of reelection and usually a gain. Similarly, maintaining strategies always exist even though they may coincide with maximizing strategies at times. By the intelligent exercise of maximizing and maintaining strategies, a representative can render his seat safe and maintain it in that condition. As we

[e]The Laplace Principle of Insufficient Reason is a classical procedure for decision making under uncertainty. According to this principle, if one is totally uncertain about the probabilities of future states of the world, one should assume they are equiprobable. In the case of independent c_j the Laplace Principle is equivalent to assuming $c_j = c_k = .5, \forall_{j,k}$.

shall see, such a happy situation does not always exist in conflictual constituencies. For this reason such districts tend to be competitive.

Roll-Call Voting Decisions with a Conflictual Constituency and Highly Salient Issues

From a situation of blissful constituency harmony, we now move to one of deep constituency division. Two significant groups hold opposing preferences on a highly salient issue. What kind of voting should one anticipate from a representative of this heterogeneous constituency? His voting decision problem appears in Table 3-2.

Let us assume the representative is certain that the groups care; i.e., $c_1 = c_2 = c = 1$. Moreover, let us begin by assuming the groups are evenly matched; i.e., $S_1 = S_2$. This special case poses a quandary for the representative. If faced with many decisions like this, he cannot long survive in the electoral area.

Consider first the maximizer. His expected return from a_1 is $c(x_1 - z_2)$, and from a_2, $c(-z_1 + x_2)$. From the identity, $S_j = (x_j + z_j)$, one sees that $c(x_1 - z_2) = c(-z_1 + x_2)$. Thus, $E(a_1) = E(a_2)$. Both strategies yield the same payoff. Furthermore, that payoff is nonpositive.

Proof

Assume the contrary: $E(a_1) = E(a_2) > 0$.

Then $\quad cx_1 > cz_2 \qquad$ (a)

and $\quad cx_2 > cz_1 \qquad$ (b)

Applying the assumption that $z_j \geq x_j$ to (a) and (b),

Table 3-2
Voting Decision Given a Two-Group Conflictual Constituency

Strategy \ State (Probability)	$G_1 G_2$ $c_1 c_2$	$G_1 \sim G_2$ $c_1(1 - c_2)$	$\sim G_1 G_2$ $(1 - c_1) c_2$	$\sim G_1 \sim G_2$ $(1 - c_1)(1 - c_2)$
with G_1	$x_1 - z_2$	x_1	$-z_2$	0
against G_1	$-z_1 + x_2$	$-z_1$	x_2	0

$$cz_1 \geqslant cx_1 > cz_2 \qquad \text{(c)}$$

$$cz_2 \geqslant cx_2 > cz_1 \qquad \text{(d)}$$

(c) and (d) are contradictory, thereby falsifying the hypothesis that $E(a_1)$ and $E(a_2)$ are both equal and positive. One sees then that the maximizer finds himself in a situation in which maximizing has a trivial meaning. His strategies are equivalent in yielding the same nonpositive expected value. Only if $z_1 = x_1 = z_2 = x_2$ will the maximizer's probability of reelection not fall ($E(a_1) = E(a_2)$ = 0). In all other cases the expected values of his strategies are negative.

Similarly, the fact that $E(a_1) = E(a_2) \leqslant 0$ implies that a maintaining strategy exists in only one special case, namely, if $z_1 = x_1 = z_2 = x_2$ which implies that no matter what the maintainer does, he just exactly breaks even: every strategy is a maintaining strategy. In all other cases no maintaining strategy exists; i.e., the maintainer cannot maintain. He loses.

So, one sees that in an evenly divided, polarized constituency, neither maximizer nor maintainer usually can expect anything but a decline in his subjective probability of reelection. In this special case all voting strategies yield identical, generally unsatisfactory payoffs. A representative who faced such decisions continually inevitably would be defeated.

But, let us proceed to the more general case of $S_1 \neq S_2$. As specified in Chapter 2, assume that the groups are ordered from stronger to weaker; i.e., ($z_1 + x_1$) > ($z_2 + x_2$). The ambiguity of the equal strength case now disappears, particularly for the maximizer. One can show easily that $E(a_1) > E(a_2)$ thereby implying that a maximizer always should vote with the stronger group.

Proof

$$E(a_1) - E(a_2) = cx_1 - cz_2 - cx_2 + cz_1$$

$$= c(S_1 - S_2)$$

which of course is positive if $S_1 > S_2$.

Note that the maximizing strategy is not necessarily a profitable one. That is, although $E(a_1) > E(a_2)$, $E(a_1)$ may be negative. In such a case the maximizing strategy is simply a loss-minimization strategy—the lesser of two evils. Thus, given high-issue salience, even unequal group strength is not sufficient to get the maximizer out of the woods. By now, some implications for the voting behavior of marginal representatives are emerging, but we will delay a discussion until analyzing the behavior of the maintainer.

Given that $c_1 = c_2 = 1$, and $S_1 > S_2$, Equation (3.3) is the maintaining strategy

$$Q = \frac{z_1 - x_2}{z_1 - x_2 + x_1 - z_2} \tag{3.3}$$

Existence is the first question of interest, In order for a maintaining strategy to exist, one must have

$$0 \leqslant \frac{z_1 - x_2}{z_1 - x_2 + x_1 - z_2} \leqslant 1$$

Given the assumption that $z_j \geqslant x_j$, the preceding condition holds if and only if condition (3.4) holds

$$x_1 \geqslant z_2 \tag{3.4}$$

From condition (3.4) one sees that even though the groups are not precisely equal in strength, if $x_1 < z_2$, the maintainer has no maintaining strategy. In fact, under certain conditions no maintaining strategies may exist even if the groups are not nearly comparable in strength. For example, if a strong group practices retribution (z_1 large) but not reward (x_1 small), condition (3.4) may not be met, even though the opposing group is rather weak. But despite a number of possible empirical interpretations the relation $x_1 < z_2$ provides a general indicator of the constituency conditions which make life difficult for maintainers. Note that if $x_1 = z_2$, $Q = 1$; i.e., maintaining and maximizing coincide.

Given that a maintaining strategy does exist in the $S_1 > S_2$ case, what can one say about it? First, Q is greater than one-half.

Proof

By Assumption,

(a) $z_1 \geqslant x_1$

(b) $z_2 \geqslant x_2$.

Given that condition (3.4) holds, (a) and (b) imply (c):

(c) $z_1 \geqslant x_1 \geqslant z_2 \geqslant x_2$,   (where at least one inequality is strict because $S_1 > S_2$)

therefore

(d) $(z_1 - x_2) > (x_1 - z_2)$.

Adding $(z_1 - x_2)$ to both sides of (d),

$$\text{(e)} \quad 2(z_1 - x_2) > (x_1 - z_2) + (z_1 - x_2).$$

Clearly, any positive fraction with the right-hand member of (e) as the denominator will be greater than a fraction having the same numerator but the left-hand member of (e) in the denominator. In particular,

$$Q = \frac{z_1 - x_2}{(x_1 - z_2) + (z_1 - x_2)} > \frac{z_1 - x_2}{2(z_1 - x_2)} = \frac{1}{2}. \quad \text{Q.E.D.}$$

So, if a maintaining strategy exists in the conflictual, high-salience case, that strategy establishes a lower bound on the representative's voting such that he always votes for the stronger group with probability greater than one-half. Depending upon the payoff values, he may have much voting freedom, or he may have little. Unfortunately, though, one can draw no firm conclusion about this matter, for Q does not vary uniformly with variations in group strength. Consider the following examples:

1. $\quad z_1 = .15 \qquad\qquad\qquad\qquad z_2 = .15$

$\qquad\quad x_1 = .15 \qquad\qquad\qquad\qquad x_2 = .14$

$\qquad\quad S_1 = .30 \qquad\qquad\qquad\qquad S_2 = .29$

$$\therefore S_1 - S_2 = .01$$

$$Q = \frac{.15 - .14}{.15 - .15 + .15 - .14} = 1.0$$

2.

$\qquad\quad z_1 = .40 \qquad\qquad\qquad\qquad z_2 = .15$

$\qquad\quad x_1 = .35 \qquad\qquad\qquad\qquad x_2 = .15$

$\qquad\quad S_1 = .75 \qquad\qquad\qquad\qquad S_2 = .30$

$$\therefore S_1 - S_2 = .40$$

$$Q = \frac{.40 - .15}{.35 - .15 + .40 - .15} = .56$$

Under case 1 above the groups are as closely matched as is possible (to two decimal places), given $z_j \geqslant x_j$ and condition (3.4). In this situation a maintainer must vote exclusively with the slightly stronger group. Under case 2 above one group is two and one-half times stronger than the other. Yet in this case a maintainer must vote with the stronger group only with some probability $\geq .56$.

According to some traditional arguments, representatives from closely divided districts take moderate, middle-of-the-road positions.[f] We have seen already that if $c_1 = c_2 = 1$, maximizers vote exclusively with the stronger group, in apparent conflict with a spirit of moderation. The preceding examples show that maintainers too, may violate the traditional arguments. In case 1, maintaining requires a representative to adopt a maximizing strategy—a certain vote with the stronger group—even though the weaker group has 97 percent as much strength as the stronger one. In case 2, on the other hand, the weaker group has only 40 percent as much strength as the stronger one, yet the representative can afford to adopt what might be viewed as a moderate voting strategy: voting with the stronger group with probability .56 and with the weaker group with probability .44.

As mentioned, however, Q does not vary uniformly with the difference in strength of the two groups.[g] Rather, Q varies oppositely with the component x_j, z_j of each S_j. Thus, which components of group strength give rise to the disparity in group strength make a great deal of difference. Generally, Q decreases as x_1 increases and decreases or remains constant as x_2 increases. As z_1 increases, Q increases or remains constant, while as z_2 increases, Q increases. Thus, to predict variations in Q from variations in group strength alone is impossible. One needs to know, in addition, the relative influence of positive and negative aspects of group strength. But one might bear in mind the example which shows that maintainers from conflictual districts may be more closely bound to the stronger group if it is barely stronger than its opposition than if it is overwhelmingly stronger.

At this point let us summarize our conclusions about representatives' voting behavior given highly salient issues and conflictual districts.

1. If contending groups are equally matched, maximizers can only minimize their losses, and maintainers generally cannot maintain.
2. If contending groups are not equally matched, maximizers vote always with the stronger group, although a positive payoff is not guaranteed. Maintaining strategies still may not exist, but if they do, the maintainer will vote with the stronger group with probability greater than one-half.
3. Given $x_1 > z_2$; as the threat potential (z_i) of either group increases, the probability a maintainer must vote with the stronger group increases. But that

[f]See Chapter 1.

[g]This fact establishes a difference between the maintaining model and Huntington's theory discussed in Chapter 1. Huntington seems to assert that there is an inverse monotonic relationship between the constituency parties' strength differential and their policy differential. We find no uniform relationship in the maintainer model.

probability declines as the reward potential (x_i) of *either* group increases. If $x_1 = z_2$, Q equals one.

4. Maintainer voting does not vary monotonically with the disparity in strength of the contending groups. Maximizer voting does not vary at all with the strength disparity.

Finally, we make the obvious point that the preceding conclusions apply anytime $c_1 = c_2$ regardless of whether they equal one. That is, equality of the c_i insures their irrelevance for voting behavior in the model. If a new issue arises for which a representative is completely uncertain about the likely constituency impact, he might presume that groups are just as likely to care as not to care (a version of Laplace's Principle). This presumption on his part would lead him to vote exactly the same way as he would were he certain that constituency groups cared ($c_j = 1, \forall_j$). Thus, within the present model, we continue to find special cases in which a concerned, issue-conscious constituency is not a necessary condition for constituency influence.

In considering the implications of the analysis for the voting behavior of representatives from marginal districts, we emphasize two points. First, because of the heterogeneous character of their districts, marginal representatives may find themselves in "can't win" situations. No matter how careful they try to be in voting, they sometimes will be unable to prevent their probability of reelection from declining. Thus, the model provides a simple and plausible explanation for the empirical correspondence between district marginality and district heterogeneity. The heterogeneous structure of the district renders it much more difficult for a representative to use his vote profitably than if the district usually has a consensual configuration. Marginality does not produce a relatively high vote of electoral defeat. Rather, heterogeneity produces both marginality and turnover in office.

Second, we find no general tendency for representatives from closely divided districts to adopt moderate, compromise positions. In fact, if the district group structure stays basically the same from issue to issue, maximizers would show anything but compromise positions. Instead they would be voting exclusively with the stronger group. On the other hand, with a highly fluid group structure, one could imagine situations in which voting with the stronger group on each issue could result in an overall record which appeared moderate. For maintainers the situation is even less determinate. In order to predict, one needs to know the values of x_1, z_1, x_2, z_2.

Throughout this section we have assumed that $c_1 = c_2$. Either the representative was certain significant groups cared about the issue, or he was so uncertain of their concern that he presumed they were just as likely to care as not to care. Much of empirical reality no doubt lies between these two poles. So, we now turn to voting decisions given a conflictual constituency when the c_i are not equal.

Roll-Call Voting Decisions with a
Conflictual Constituency

If two significant conflicting groups have unequal probabilities of caring, the voting strategies representatives must adopt are dependent on the magnitudes of those probabilities. Naturally, two cases arise. In the first, the stronger group has a higher probability of caring. The second case is reminiscent of a classic subject in democratic theory: the intensity problem.[1] The group that can do less to the representative's probability of reelection than its opposition has a greater likelihood of doing so.[h] We will take both cases in turn for maximizers and then for maintainers.

Because $E(a_1) = (c_1x_1 - c_2z_2)$, and $E(a_2) = (-c_1z_1 + c_2x_2)$, one sees that $E(a_1) - E(a_2) = (c_1S_1 - c_2S_2)$. By the ordering of groups from stronger to weaker, $S_1 \geqslant S_2$. Thus, $E(a_1) > E(a_2)$ if $c_1 > c_2$. The latter would be a sufficient condition for the maximizer's choice of a_1. But even if $c_1 \leqslant c_2$, $E(a_1)$ may be greater than $E(a_2)$ if S_1 exceeds S_2 sufficiently that $c_1S_1 > c_2S_2$. Thus our condition should be more precise. A necessary and sufficient condition for $E(a_1) > E(a_2)$ is simply

$$c_1/c_2 > S_2/S_1 \qquad (3.5)$$

That is, even if $c_1 < c_2$, the maximizer still chooses to vote with the stronger group if c_1 is closer in magnitude to c_2 than the strength of the weaker group is to the strength of the stronger group.

In exactly parallel fashion the maximizer votes with the weaker group if

$$c_1/c_2 < S_2/S_1 \qquad (3.6)$$

Naturally, if $c_1/c_2 = S_2/S_1$, $E(a_1) = E(a_2)$ and the maximizer is indifferent between his two strategies. Note that if $c_1 = c_2$, (3.5) summarizes our conclusions about maximizer voting in the previous section.

Thus, where the c_i are not equal, they are relevant for voting behavior. In particular, a group may use its high potential to make a campaign issue out of a vote to offset its strength disadvantage on the vote. If a representative estimates that $c_i = 1.0$ for a local sportsmen's club on a gun-control vote and miniscule for

---

[h]One should be aware that there are differences between the concepts utilized in our analysis and those used in the debate about the intensity problem. For example, we speak of strong and weak groups but do not necessarily equate these with the majorities and minorities of democratic theory. Money can affect p as well as numbers. Additionally, the probability estimate that a group cares seems more a measure of salience than one of intensity, though the two concepts clearly are related. Actually, "intensity" is one of the most difficult of all social science concepts to get a grip on. For discussions, see Alvin Rabushka and Kenneth Shepsle, *A Theory of Democratic Instability* (Columbus: Merrill, 1972), Chapter 2; Douglas Rae and Michael Taylor, *The Analysis of Political Cleavages* (New Haven: Yale, 1970), Chapter 3.

everyone else, maximizing may dictate voting with the hunters despite their small numbers. Of course, we observe such behavior regularly in real world legislatures.

Maximizer voting varies with changes in the c_i exactly as one would expect. Recall again that $E(a_1) = (c_1 x_1 - c_2 z_2)$, while $E(a_2) = (-c_1 z_1 + c_2 x_2)$. As c_1 increases, $E(a_1)$ increases or remains constant while $E(a_2)$ falls. This implies that as c_1 increases the likelihood that $E(a_1) > E(a_2)$ increases.[i] The higher the probability that the stronger group cares, the greater the likelihood the maximizer finds voting with them to be his optimal strategy. Conversely, as c_2 increases, $E(a_1)$ decreases while $E(a_2)$ increases or remains constant. This implies that as c_2 increases the likelihood that $E(a_1) < E(a_2)$ increases. The higher the probability that the weaker group cares the more likely is the maximizer to find voting with them his optimal strategy. Whatever one's position on the justice of the matter, maximizers in the model "weigh votes as well as count them."

For maintainers, (3.7) is the maintaining strategy in the unequal c_i case. Of course, if $c_1 = c_2$ (3.7)

$$Q = \frac{c_1 z_1 - c_2 x_2}{c_1 z_1 - c_2 x_2 + c_1 x_1 - c_2 z_2} \tag{3.7}$$

reduces to (3.3). Again, we must ascertain the conditions under which $0 \leqslant Q \leqslant 1.0$. Unlike the earlier case of condition (3.4), the unequal c_i case gives rise to two conditions. A first sufficient condition for the existence of a maintaining strategy is

$$c_1 x_1 \geqslant c_2 z_2 \qquad \text{or} \qquad c_1/c_2 \geqslant z_2/x_1 \tag{3.8}$$

This condition insures that the numerator of (3.7) is nonnegative (because $z_j \geqslant x_j, \forall_j$) and less than or equal to the denominator. Therefore, $0 \leqslant Q \leqslant 1$. But there also exists another sufficient condition for the existence of a maintaining strategy:

$$c_1 z_1 \leqslant c_2 x_2 \qquad \text{or} \qquad c_1/c_2 \leqslant x_2/z_1, \tag{3.9}$$

Condition (3.9) insures that the numerator of (3.7) is nonpositive and greater than or equal to the denominator (also nonpositive). But then the absolute value of the numerator is less than or equal to the absolute value of the denominator and cancellation of the minus signs yields $0 \leqslant Q \leqslant 1$.

---

[i]Strictly speaking, of course, $E(a_1)$ either will or will not be greater than $E(a_2)$. Thus, we use the term "likelihood" in the sense in which it is used in statistics. From an a priori standpoint, high c_1 and low c_2 make it more likely that $E(a_1) > E(a_2)$. Low c_1 and high c_2 make it more likely that $E(a_2) > E(a_1)$.

The two sufficient conditions, (3.8) and (3.9), establish bounds on the ratio c_1/c_2. Specifically, they show that no maintaining strategy exists if

$$x_2/z_1 < c_1/c_2 < z_2/x_1 \tag{3.10}$$

Thus we arrive at a necessary and sufficient condition for the existence of a maintaining strategy in somewhat roundabout fashion: c_1/c_2 must not fall inside the open interval given by (3.10).

One can more readily examine the conditions for the existence of maintaining strategies if we divide these strategies into two classes. We say that a representative has a Type I maintaining strategy if the first sufficient condition (3.8) holds. Similarly, a representative has a Type II maintaining strategy if the second sufficient condition (3.9) holds. Then we can say that inequalities (3.8) and (3.9) are necessary and sufficient conditions for the existence of Type I and Type II maintaining strategies, respectively.

Since the preceding discussion may have seemed rather abstract, we present some fictional decision problems in Table 3-3. In the first case we illustrate a Type I maintaining strategy, $c_1/c_2 = 6/3$, which satisfies (3.8), or alternately, exceeds the upper bound given in (3.10). In case 2, $c_1/c_2 = 1/6$, which satisfies (3.9), or, alternatively, falls below the lower bound in (3.10). Thus we have a Type II maintaining strategy. In case 3, $c_1/c_2 = 3/6$, which lies within the crucial interval (3.10). In this situation no optimal strategy exists. The attempted calculation leads to an absurdity: $Q = -1.0$.

Obviously, the appearance of the c_i in the maintainer's decision rule yields some results which differ from those of the earlier analysis. We have seen three such differences already. First, even if the groups are so closely matched that a maintaining strategy would not exist in the equal c_i case, the maintainer has an optimal strategy if his estimate of the probability the stronger group cares sufficiently exceeds his estimate of the probability the weaker group cares to render $c_1 x_1 \geqslant c_2 z_2$.

Second, we have seen that even if the above condition does not hold, the legislator's estimate of c_1 may be sufficiently small and/or the estimate of c_2 sufficiently large that both the numerator and denominator of Q are negative. Thus the maintainer has the possibility of satisfying his reelection goal by heeding the wishes of a concerned few, if they exist.

Third, we have seen that in an example of the case just discussed, $Q = .11$. This indicates that our analysis in the preceding section does not extend to the general case. In fact, it is the case that if a maintaining strategy exists via satisfaction of the Type II sufficient condition, $Q \leqslant .5$. To see this, consider the following:

From (3.9), if a Type II maintaining strategy exists

$$c_1 z_1 - c_2 x_2 = -\epsilon \qquad \text{where } \epsilon \geqslant 0$$

Table 3-3
Decision Problems Illustrating the Conditions for the Existence of Maintaining Strategies

Case 1.		
	$x_1 = .2$	$x_2 = .1$
	$z_1 = .4$	$z_2 = .3$
	$c_1 = .6$	$c_2 = .3$

$c_1/c_2 = 6/3 > 3/2 = z_2/x_1$. ∴ A Type I Strategy Exists

$Q = .88$

Case 2.		
	$x_1 = .2$	$x_2 = .1$
	$z_1 = .4$	$z_2 = .3$
	$c_1 = .1$	$c_2 = .6$

$c_1/c_2 = 1/6 < 1/4 = x_2/z_1$. ∴ A Type II Strategy Exists

$Q = .11$

Case 3.		
	$x_1 = .2$	$x_2 = .1$
	$z_1 = .4$	$z_2 = .3$
	$c_1 = .3$	$c_2 = .6$

$x_2/z_1 = 1/4 < 3/6 = c_1/c_2 < 3/2 = z_2/x_1$. Therefore, no maintaining strategy exists for this decision.

$Q = -1.0$ which contradicts the definition of Q as a probability,

$$0 \leqslant Q \leqslant 1$$

By assumption $z_j \geqslant x_j, \forall_j$. Therefore,

$$(c_1 x_1 - c_2 z_2) \leqslant (c_1 z_1 - c_2 x_2) = -\epsilon$$

∴ let $(c_1 x_1 - c_2 z_2) = -(\epsilon + \Delta)$ where $\Delta \geqslant 0$

Then

$$Q = \frac{-\epsilon}{-(\epsilon + \Delta) - \epsilon} = \frac{-\epsilon}{-(2\epsilon + \Delta)} \leqslant 1/2 \qquad \text{Q.E.D.}$$

Thus, where a Type II maintaining strategy exists, it will specify that the representative vote with the *weaker* group with probability at least .5.

As one might expect, Type I maintaining strategies specify that a representative vote with the *stronger* group with probability at least .5.[j] The proof parallels the above.

Thus, the behavior of maintainers, too, may reflect a weighing of preferences as well as counting of them. But before theoretical confirmation of our common sense notions makes us too sanguine, let us examine the maintaining strategies more fully. Specifically, how does Q vary as c_1 and c_2 vary? Because Q is meaningful only within a certain range and contains several discontinuities and "steps," one must exercise care in differentiating this function. But differentiating within "smooth" and substantively meaningful ranges, we have the following facts:

$$\frac{\partial Q}{\partial c_1} = \frac{[c_1(x_1 + z_1) - c_2(z_2 + x_2)]z_1 - (c_1z_1 - c_2x_2)(z_1 + x_1)}{[c_1(x_1 + z_1) - c_2(x_2 + z_2)]^2}$$

$$= \frac{c_1x_1z_1 + c_1z_1^2 - c_2z_2z_1 - c_2x_2z_1 - c_1z_1^2 + c_2x_2z_1 - c_1z_1x_1 + c_2x_2x_1}{[c_1(x_1 + z_1) - c_2(x_2 + z_2)]^2}$$

$$= \frac{c_2x_2x_1 - c_2z_2z_1}{[c_1(x_1 + z_1) - c_2(x_2 + z_2)]^2} \leqslant 0 \text{ because } z_j \geqslant x_j, \forall j.$$

$$\frac{\partial Q}{\partial c_2} = \frac{[c_1(x_1 + z_1) - c_2(x_2 + z_2)](-x_2) - (c_1z_1 - c_2x_2)[-(z_2 + x_2)]}{[c_1(x_1 + z_1) - c_2(x_2 + z_2)]^2}$$

$$= \frac{-c_1x_1x_2 - c_1z_1x_2 + c_2x_2^2 + c_2x_2z_2 + c_1z_1z_2 - c_2x_2z_2 + c_1z_1x_2 - c_2x_2^2}{[c_1(x_1 + z_1) - c_2(x_2 + z_2)]^2}$$

$$= \frac{c_1z_1z_2 - c_1x_1x_2}{[c_1(x_1 + z_1) - c_2(x_2 + z_2)]^2} \geqslant 0 \text{ because } z_j \geqslant x_j, \forall j.$$

So, as c_1 increases, Q decreases or remains constant, while as c_2 increases, Q increases or remains constant. Amazingly, in the maintainer model with a two-group, heterogeneous constituency, as the probability that the stronger group cares increases, the minimum probability, Q, that the representative must vote with them *decreases or stays constant*. Conversely, as the probability that the weaker group cares increases, the maximum probability $(1 - Q)$ that the representative can vote with them *decreases or stays constant*. Thus, the c_j affect

[j]Note that in the equal c_i case *only* Type I maintaining strategies exist (except in the special case of $x_1 = z_1 = z_2 = x_2$ which makes all strategies maintaining strategies and the denominator of (3.7) zero).

a maintainer's voting in the model precisely opposite to the manner in which they affect a maximizer's voting. In the model, if one's representative is a maintainer, to cause him to raise his estimate that you care may be to work against yourself. Two examples will illustrate this phenomenon.

Example 1: Type I Maintaining Strategy

let $x_1 = .15$ $\qquad\qquad$ $x_2 = .05$

$\quad\ \ z_1 = .30$ $\qquad\qquad$ $z_2 = .10$

Case A.) $c_1 = .4$
$\qquad\quad c_2 = .4$ $\qquad\qquad$ $Q = \dfrac{.12 - .02}{.18 - .06} = .83$

Case B.) $c_1 = 1.0$
$\qquad\quad c_2 = .4$ $\qquad\qquad$ $Q = \dfrac{.30 - .02}{.45 - .06} = .72$

Case C.) $c_1 = .4$
$\qquad\quad c_2 = .6$ $\qquad\qquad$ $Q = \dfrac{.12 - .03}{.18 - .09} = 1.0$

Thus, as c_1 increases (.4 to 1.0), Q decreases (.83 to .72). Conversely, as c_2 increases (.4 to .6), Q increases (.83 to 1.0). By effecting an increase in c_1 the stronger group only increases their representative's voting latitude. By effecting an increase in c_2 the weaker group only drives the representative more closely into the arms of the opposition.

Example 2: Type II Maintaining Strategy.

let $x_1 = .24$ $\qquad\qquad$ $x_2 = .20$

$\quad\ \ z_1 = .30$ $\qquad\qquad$ $z_2 = .25$

Case A.) $c_1 = .3$
$\qquad\quad c_2 = .6$ $\qquad\qquad$ $Q = \dfrac{.09 - .12}{.165 - .270} = \dfrac{-.03}{-.105} = .29$

Case B.) $c_1 = .4$
$\qquad\quad c_2 = .6$ $\qquad\qquad$ $Q = \dfrac{.12 - .12}{.22 - .27} = 0$

Case C.) $c_1 = .3$
$\qquad\quad c_2 = 1.0$ $\qquad\qquad$ $Q = \dfrac{.09 - .20}{.154 - .45} = \dfrac{-.11}{-.285} = .39$

Thus, as c_1 increases (.3 to .4), Q decreases (.29 to 0), while as c_2 increases (.6 to 1.0), Q increases (.29 to .39). Again the raises in c_i lead to counterproductive results from the standpoint of constituents. If the maintainer model has any resemblance to reality, findings attesting to voter ignorance may not illustrate irrational or even nonrational behavior; quite the contrary. To communicate with one's representative before a vote might backfire if he happens to be a maintainer.

There is, however, one fairly important qualification to the preceding remarks. Sufficiently large increases in the c_i may alter the strategic situation which exists; i.e., to one of no maintaining strategy, or from a Type I to a Type II strategy or vice versa. If a Type I strategy exists, the stronger group should never make an effort to raise c_1, but the weaker group might try to raise c_2 in an effort to change the strategic situation; i.e., from Type I to Type II.[k] Of course, if the weaker group fails to raise c_2 enough, they may end up in a position worse than the initial one. If a Type II strategy exists, the same conclusion holds with the roles of the groups reversed.

Well, we have a logical fact that changes in the c_i produce differential changes in the numerator and denominator of (3.7). Just how meaningful is that fact? Many will find the interpretation of the mathematics so counterintuitive that they will reject it substantively without further ado. What does such a rejection imply? What assumptions are driving the maintainer model in the conflictual, unequal c_j case?

Well, to begin with the arguments just presented are not terribly robust. For example, if we go from the two-group case to the n-group case with two or more contending groups on each side, Q may increase, decrease, or stay constant as any particular c_j varies. Similarly, if we do not assume independent c_j, the dependence of Q on the c_j is indeterminate. Finally, if we allow the c_j to be dependent on the x_j and z_j, we cannot make the *ceteris paribus* assumption necessary for partial differentiation. Thus, one or more of the simplifying assumptions utilized in the analysis may be giving rise to the peculiar behavioral pattern found in the model world. As these assumptions are relaxed, unusual substantive conclusions may disappear. Still, the counterintuitive conclusions simply give way to indeterminate situations as we relax assumptions. Given

---

[k]To elaborate, if a Type I maintaining strategy exists (i.e., if $c_1 x_1 \geq c_2 z_2$), Q increases toward 1.0 as c_2 increases. But if it is possible; i.e., if $c_2 < 1$, for c_2 to increase to the point that $c_1 x_1 < c_2 z_2$, Q becomes at first greater than 1. Since Q is a probability restricted to the interval $[0, 1]$, we consider Q undefined at these values of c_2. Nevertheless, if c_2 continues to increase, at some value the negative term ($c_1 x_1 - c_2 z_2$) may equal the positive term ($c_1 z_1 - c_2 x_2$). At this value of c_2, the denominator of Q is zero—a mathematical discontinuity. Beyond this point Q is negative for a time—again a defined discontinuity. Finally, if it is possible for c_2 to increase still more, we may reach the point where $c_1 z_1 \leq c_2 x_2$, the realm of the Type II maintaining strategy, whereupon Q leaps into the interval $[0, .5]$, and then increases to .5 if a further increase is possible; i.e., if c_2 still is less than one.

particular values of the theoretical variables the counterintuitive dependence of Q on the c_j may still hold. Given other values, common sense conclusions may follow.

Simplifying assumptions aside, the maintaining notion itself probably bears much of the responsibility for any surprising analytic implications. After all, even in the presence of simplifying assumptions the maximizing notion produced no jarring conclusions. To digress momentarily, we have investigated a variant of the maintainer model in which p^* remains forever constant rather than "tracking" p. Thus, a representative typically finds himself an amount, v, away from p^* and votes so as to return to p^* on each vote. In that variant if v is positive, $\partial Q/\partial c_1$, is strictly negative, while $\partial Q/\partial c_2$ is indeterminate. If v is negative, $\partial Q/\partial c_1$ is indeterminate while $\partial Q/\partial c_2$ is strictly positive. Perhaps it is the case that satisficing models simply will produce some strange consequences when applied to real situations even if few simplifying assumptions are present.

Of course, there is one further possibility: namely, that the peculiar behavior observed in the model actually occurs empirically. More than a few observers have noted that pressure can be counterproductive.[2] Consider the familiar "profiles in courage" on the part of our representatives. A highly controversial bill will come to the floor for a vote. Various interests carry out active lobbying, a few dire threats are heard, and, no doubt, someone rises in debate to say that in all his ___ years in _____ , he has never seen such intense, unashamed pressure politics. But in the end, some representatives bravely stride forth apparently to vote their consciences and/or the public interest. Without downplaying entirely courage, integrity, and other admirable qualities, one might note that in the model world, such activities are far less dangerous and thus less courageous than they appear. Take, for example, organized labor's intensive lobbying effort during passage of the Landrum-Griffin Bill in 1959. Supposing that labor is the weaker group (vis-à-vis management) in most Republican constituencies, by threatening Republican Congressmen, labor only was lessening the probability that Republicans could vote against the bill. And, in taking an antilabor stand in the face of fierce pressure, Republican Congressmen's courageous behavior happened to coincide with allowable voting according to our analysis.[3] In view of the not-infrequent occurrence of incidents like this, perhaps the conclusions of the conflictual two-group maintainer model should not be dismissed so quickly.

In any case, we do not regret the opposite conclusions the analysis implies about the effects of varying c_i on maximizer and maintainer voting. At best, the conclusions are empirically accurate, in which case we have learned an extremely interesting fact about legislative behavior. At worst, one set of conclusions (most likely about the maintainer) is empirically wrong, in which case we have some idea of which theoretical ideas deserve no further attention. Either way, we have increased our knowledge.

To summarize then, the analysis implies the following conclusions about voting behavior in the two-group conflictual case:

1. When $c_1 \geqslant c_2$ maximizers vote exclusively with the stronger group: if $c_1 < c_2$ they may switch allegiance to the weaker group if (3.6) holds. In neither case will the vote necessarily result in a nonnegative change in probability of reelection.
2. Maintaining strategies may not exist. If a Type I strategy exists, a maintainer must vote with the stronger group with probability at least .5. If a Type II strategy exists, a maintainer must vote with the weaker group with probability at least .5.
3. As the probability that a group cares increases the likelihood that a maximizer votes with them also increases. But for maintainers the opposite is true. As the probability that a group cares increases, the probability that a maintainer must vote with them decreases or remains constant.
4. Maximizer voting varies with group strength only to the extent that (3.5) or (3.6) holds. Maintainer voting varies with group strength in no consistent pattern.

Overall, we find that in the general case of the two-group conflictual constituency the previous implications for the voting behavior of marginal representatives are reinforced. Maximizing strategies may involve choosing the least damaging position. Maintaining strategies may not exist. Whether the c_i are equal or unequal, high or low, representatives may not be able to use their votes to increase their probabilities of reelection. Thus, a representative whose district customarily displays heterogeneity of interests will face a more difficult task in casting his roll-call votes than a representative whose district customarily displays homogeneity of interests. Again, heterogeneity makes marginality more likely.

Implications

In this chapter we have examined a simple model of constituency influence on representative' roll-call voting. Our primary effort has been to analyze and compare voting decisions given consensual or conflictual constituency configurations. In this concluding section we wish to discuss some implications of the analysis for the study of constituency influence.

We will only briefly mention a persistent theme of the chapter. Because of the structure of the respective decision problems, representatives whose districts tend to be consensual on most votes can render and maintain their seats safe by voting intelligently. Conversely, representatives whose districts tend to be conflictual on most votes may have no way (within the model) to increase or maintain their probabilities of reelection. They are between the proverbial fire and frying pan. Thus, the model provides a simple explanation for the oft-noted empirical correspondence between district homogeneity and electoral safety on the one hand, and district heterogeneity and electoral marginality on the other. Enough said, until Chapter 5.

One of the general implications of the model is extremely significant for the interpretations of existing empirical studies of constituency influence on roll-call voting. Recall that roll-call voting behavior in the model does not vary in any nice linear fashion with group strength. Let us push this finding a bit. Consider a group of representatives who vote on a number of similar labor bills and estimate that c_L for labor equals c_B for business on each bill. Now, assume that some constituency demographic characteristic (e.g., percent blue collar) correlates perfectly with group strength in the district. Thus, in districts which include 0 to x percent blue collar, labor is the weaker group, while in districts which include x to 100 percent blue collar, labor is the stronger group. How will our sample of model representatives behave? For maximizers the theoretical pattern will appear as in Figure 3-1. For maintainers the pattern will appear as in Figure 3-2. Now, if one were to regress labor support on percent blue collar, what would the statistics show? For maximizers, maintainers, or any mixture of the two, linear regression would estimate a positive relationship but a poor fit—exactly what numerous empirical studies show. Furthermore, if some dichotomous variable (e.g., party?) were highly correlated with labor's position as the stronger or weaker constituency group, then controlling for that variable would result in no statistical relationship within subgroups for maximizers and only coincidental relationships for maintainers. Thus, in our model—*a model in which constituency is the primary influence on legislative voting behavior*—the application of commonly used statistical techniques would lead to the erroneous

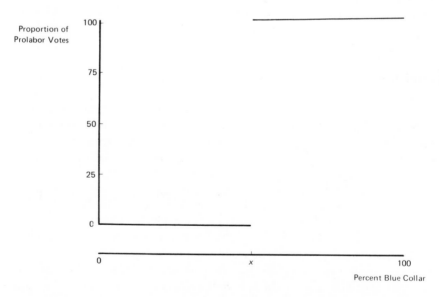

Figure 3-1. Predicted Proportion of Prolabor Votes by Maximizers.

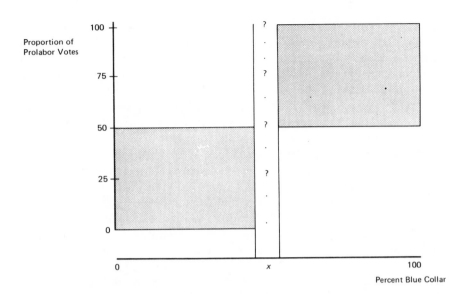

Figure 3-2. Predicted Proportion of Prolabor Votes by Maintainers.*
*The exact locations of data points within the Northeast and Southwest quadrants depends on the particular values of the x_i, z_i. A priori there is no reason to expect any given patterning rather than another.

conclusion that at best, constituency influence operates through the party medium, and at worst, that no constituency influence exists.[1] Too often researchers write as if the only alternative to a linear relationship were no relationship. But statistical models applied to data contain implicit behavioral models. If these implicit models are wrong, the substantive conclusions drawn are likely to be wrong also.

On a more positive note, the model provides a number of testable propositions, although data difficulties cannot be minimized. Of course, our conclusions do not resemble the "simple" familiar empirical propositions. Nowhere do we hypothesize that "scores on scale x increase monotonically with percent urban

---

[1]For those not familiar with the statistical analyses referred to, we present an example. Using simple linear regression, we have estimated the relationship between AFL-CIO COPE scores and percent blue collar in 323 non-Southern Congressional districts for the 88th Congress. According to traditional hypotheses, support for organized labor will increase as the proportion of blue collar workers in a district increases. Such in fact is the case: $Y = 37.05 + 1.42X$, $R^2 = .09$, a weak relationship to be sure, but not atypical of those political scientists ordinarily find. Yet when we split the data set by party, for Republicans ($n = 171$) we get $Y = 10.8 + .27X$, $R^2 = .01$, while for Democrats ($n = 157$) we get $Y = 77.05 + .31X$, $R^2 = .04$, negligible relationships. Thus the typical conclusion: controlling for party eliminates the appearance of constituency influence. But we know that percent blue collar is related to electing Democrats rather than Republicans. Thus we have the situation discussed in the text above. If our theory were correct, constituency influence would be present but the method would not uncover it.

as defined by the Census Bureau." Instead we present the somewhat more complex relationships implied by Equation (3.7) and the discrete rather than continuous relationships predicted for maximizer voting. But any criticism on this score seems misplaced. In rationalizing why their correlational methods account for so little of the variance in roll-call voting, researchers frequently point to the "complexity" of the voting decisions—the "myriad forces which impinge upon the legislator." We too, are saying only that the relationship between constituents' preferences and the voting decision is a bit more subtle than heretofore admitted. Hypothesizing that roll-call voting is linear with demographic characteristics of constituencies is just *too* simple. At least our analysis suggests that is so.

Additionally, empirical researchers may be somewhat disappointed by the unfamiliar terms in which our conclusions are stated. We do not say that Southern Congressmen are most bound to their constituents on civil rights votes, or that mid-western Republicans are most bound on farm price support votes. Instead we speak of strong and weak groups, increasing and decreasing c_j's, etc. Searching for regularities on the level of specific groups and issues involves searching on the wrong level in our opinion. These particular groups and issues may determine the values of the x_j, z_j, and c_j. But generalizing about the values of the decision components, which may be quite variable and short-lived, seems far less profitable than generalizing about the way in which the components, whatever they are, affect the decision. If our theory is tested and not falsified, statements about Southern Democrats, mid-western Republicans, gun-control votes, foreign-aid votes, etc. may be made on the basis of the test, *but they hold only because at the time of the test they affected the theoretical variables in a particular way.* Ten years from now particular substantive statements might be reversed while the general propositions of the theory could be supported to the same degree as before.

We realize that some of the propositions advanced may strike the casual reader as rather obvious hypotheses that common sense unaided by decision theory would have suggested. Perfectly true. But a theory which implied exclusively nonobvious propositions would probably be wrong; i.e., falsified. The fact that some of the theoretical propositions appear perfectly acceptable and expected provides an indication that we are on the right track and encourages testing the less obvious implications.

Notes

1. Robert Dahl, *A Preface to Democratic Theory* (Chicago: University of Chicago Press, 1956), Chapter 4. Wilmoore Kendall and George Carey, "The Intensity Problem and Democratic Theory," *American Political Science Review*, 62 (1968), 5-25.

2. Raymond Bauer, Ithiel de Sola Pool and Lewis A. Dexter, *American Business and Public Policy* (New York: Atherton, 1968), pp. 442-443.

3. For a study of Landrum-Griffin see Samuel Patterson, *Labor Lobbying and Labor Reform* (Indianapolis: Bobbs-Merrill, 1966).

4

Extensions of the Basic Theory

Introduction

The model presented in Chapter 3 is an extremely parsimonious one, an admittedly great simplification of a representative's roll-call voting decision. Of course, there are various possibilities for making the basic model a better approximation to empirical reality. By augmenting or modifying basic assumptions one can construct a more complex but perhaps more useful model. Such changes, both actual and potential, are the concern of this chapter.

Abstention

While reading of the difficulties representatives from conflictual districts sometimes face, one naturally wonders about the merits of avoiding the situation entirely. That is, a representative's constituency may not only affect the way in which he votes, but also whether he votes at all. Thus, a reasonably complete theory of constituency influence should recognize the representative's option to abstain. Of course, on empirical grounds one might doubt that abstention is all that important. According to *Congressional Quarterly*, failure to vote in recent Congresses averages less than 20 percent, while failure to take a public position averages less than 10 percent.[1] Further, a good number of these relatively few abstentions undoubtedly do not result from considered decisions to abstain on a given vote. Rather, the Congressman might be visiting in the district, traveling, or otherwise absent for any and all votes which take place during a given time period. Still, the remaining abstentions might not be distributed at all randomly. Possibly abstention is an important, though seldom-used strategy. Furthermore, abstention might occur precisely in those situations identified as most difficult in the earlier analysis. Thus, conscious abstentions might be more important than their relatively low empirical frequency would suggest. Not that this is necessarily our position, but we recognize the possibility.

Assume, then, that every representative perceives three available options for every roll-call vote decision. He can vote "yea," vote "nay," or abstain. If abstention is viewed as a legitimate voting strategy, then it must have reelection consequences associated with it, as do the representative's other strategies. Specifically, we incorporate abstention into our analysis via the following assumption: If $c_j > 0$ the decision to abstain is estimated to reduce the representative's subjective probability of reelection an amount y_j, where $0 < y_j \leqslant z_j, \forall G_j$.

That is, we assume that a representative estimates that an abstention when a group "cares" costs him something, but certainly no more than voting against the group. In our opinion this is the most plausible assumption one can make about abstention. Let us see where the assumption leads.

1. Abstention with a Homogeneous Constituency

Consider the expanded decision problem for the homogeneous case (Table 4-1).

Obviously, the possibility of abstention makes no difference to a maximizer. Voting with his constituents remains the dominant strategy. Thus, a maximizer from a homogeneous constituency makes no use of his abstention strategy, preferring to vote always with his constituents.

In contrast, the possibility of abstention can affect a maintainer's voting. Given that he can assign some probability, A, to his abstention strategy, the maintaining strategy, Q_A, is easily found:

$$E(\Delta p) = Q_A cx + Q_A c0 - Acy + Ac0 + (1 - Q_A - A)(-cz)$$

$$+ (1 - Q_A - A)(c0)$$

$$= Q_A cx - Acy - cz + Q_A cz + Acz$$

$$cz \quad = Q_A (cx + cz) - A(cy - cz)$$

$$\frac{z + A(y - z)}{x + z} = Q_A \tag{4.1}$$

(We have labeled the Q in (4.1) Q_A to distinguish it from the Q in (3.1)). If $A = 0$, then $Q_A = Q$. But if $A > 0$, then $Q_A \leqslant Q$ by the assumption that $y \leqslant z$. Thus

Table 4-1
Voting Decision for a Homogeneous Constituency, Three-Strategy Case

Probability State / Strategy	Cares (c)	~ Care ($1 - c$)
a_1 (with)	x	0
a_2 (abstain)	$-y$	0
a_3 (oppose)	$-z$	0

we find that in the homogeneous case, a maintainer may well be able to attain a greater degree of voting freedom by abstaining on some votes of concern to the constituency than by voting against the constituency on those votes—an entirely plausible result. Furthermore, since maximizers never abstain but maintainers may, we can draw another conclusion: given like numbers of votes on which $c_j > 0$, the number of abstentions by a maintainer is greater than or equal to the number of abstentions by a maximizer. Just what probability the maintainer should assign to his abstention strategy is a question with no pat answer. If $y = z$, a maintainer probably will not consider abstaining. For, he expects to lose as much electorally by abstaining as by voting against constituents, and no doubt, vote commitments are generally worth somewhat more in trade to fellow legislators than are agreements to abstain. Thus, should constituents have this "He who is not with us is against us" attitude, the theoretical option of abstaining most likely will not be a practical empirical option for a maintainer. On the other hand, if y is strictly less than z, a maintainer might very well scrap the "against" strategy altogether, especially if he estimates that he can use abstentions nearly as effectively as "against" votes to achieve secondary goals. Of course, even if $y < z$, the probability the maintainer can assign to his abstention strategy is not freely determined by him. In the most extreme case in which probability Q_A is assigned to a_1, $A = (1 - Q_A)$ to a_2, and 0 to a_3 it must be the case that $Q_A + A = 1$. Solving for A,

$$\frac{z + A(y - z)}{x + z} + A = 1.0$$

$$z + A(y - z) + A(x + z) = x + z$$

$$Ay - Az + Ax + Az = x$$

$$A = x/(y + x) \tag{4.2}$$

Equation (4.2) yields the upper bound for A in the one-group consensual case. Naturally, if some nonzero probability is assigned to a_3, then $A < x/(y + x)$, for, Q_A must increase to balance out the expected negative increment from using a_3, and if the probabilities assigned to a_1 and a_3 increase, evidently that assigned to a_2 must decrease. From (4.2) one sees that the smaller the maintainer's estimate of x the smaller the probability he can abstain, and the larger the maintainer's estimate of y the smaller the probability he can abstain. Most importantly, $x = 0$ implies $A = 0$. Thus, *in the situation from the two-strategy analysis in which a maintainer is most bound to the constituency (x = 0 implies Q = 1), the possibility of abstention does nothing to alleviate his bondage.* The one conclusion from Chapter 3 which does not hold if abstention is allowed is that $Q \geqslant .5$. Evidently, Q_A can be less than .5 if $y < z$, and $x \neq 0$.

Based on the analysis thus far, we offer the following conclusions about voting behavior with a consensual district:

1. Maximizers never abstain, whereas maintainers may. Thus, abstention rates among the latter will be greater than among the former given a similar number of votes for which $c_j > 0$.
2. The higher the maintainer's estimate of y (the cost of abstaining), the higher the probability he must vote with his constituents. (Unless $x = 0$, in which case $Q_A = Q = 1$)

$(\partial Q_A / \partial y \geqslant 0)$

3. The lower the maintainer's estimate of x (the reward from voting with), the lower the probability that he can abstain.

$(\partial A / \partial x > 0)$

4. If constituents have a "He who is not with us is against us" orientation ($y = z$), the possibility of abstention does not alter the minimum probability that the maintainer must vote with his constituents.

(From (4.1), $y = z$ implies $Q_A = Q$)

5. If $x = 0$ (no reward for voting with), a maintainer assigns no positive probability to his abstention strategy.

(From (4.2), $x = 0$ implies $A = 0$)

And, of course, if more than one group may care about the issue but all agree, then each of these five conclusions extends in perfectly obvious fashion to this more complex case. Note, too that even with abstention, the variable c is irrelevant to the analysis in exactly the same situations as in the two-strategy consensual case (nonzero in the one-group case, equal c_j in the more than one-group case).

At several points in our discussion we have hinted that the use of the abstention strategy depends in part on the maintainer's ability to trade *abstentions* for secondary goals vis-à-vis his ability to trade *votes*. Without abstention one assumes simply that the lower is Q the better. For, the representative can attain any secondary goal associated with voting with constituents and has a chance $(1 - Q)$ of attaining those rewards associated with voting against them. Obviously, the larger is $(1 - Q)$, the better for the maintainer. With abstention, however, one cannot claim that the lower is Q the better, without obtaining additional information. Even if $y < z$, the maintainer might choose the higher Q which results from assigning some nonzero probability to voting against his constituents over the lower Q_A which results from assigning all residual probability $(1 - Q_A)$ to his abstention strategy, if he believes that abstentions are worthless for obtaining secondary goals, but votes are not. Thus, even when $y < z$, we would hesitate to state unconditionally that maintainers from homogeneous constituencies always abstain rather than vote against constituents.

To some extent one can specify in which situations abstentions are valuable currency in horse-trading. Consider an N-person legislature that divides rather evenly between two parties. Either party leader should value the abstention of an opponent nearly as much as a vote-switch. If the party division is exactly equal, abstentions and vote-switches come close to being strategically equivalent. In such a situation we would expect maintainers from homogeneous constituencies to "take a walk" rather than vote against their people. Of course if we could formulate a way of assigning values to abstention commitments, we could be quite precise in our theoretical statements about abstaining vs. voting "against." For example, if a representative can estimate that an abstention is worth d $(0 \leqslant d \leqslant 1)$ times the trading value of a vote, then maintainers from homogeneous constituencies would abstain rather than vote against constituents so long as $z > (1/d)y$ (subject to (4.2)). In essence, if an abstention is worth say, half as much as an against vote in achieving secondary goals, a maintainer should abstain rather than vote against if $z > 2y$. In this way, given two similar votes, he achieves an equal value in secondary rewards at the cost of a smaller loss in subjective probability of reelection.

This concludes our consideration of abstention in the homogeneous case. To summarize, the possibility of abstention does not greatly alter the voting situation for the representative from a homogeneous constituency. A maximizer's voting is completely unaffected by the option to abstain. For a maintainer $Q_A < Q$ if $y < z$. If not, a maintainer's voting, too, does not change as a result of the opportunity to abstain. In the maintainer's most restricted situation in the two-strategy case ($x = 0 \rightarrow Q = 1.0$), the possibility of abstention does not give him any leeway. We conclude, then, that for the homogeneous case the theory can be extended without difficulty and without appreciably altering the simple analysis.

2. Abstention in the Heterogeneous Two-Group Constituency, $c_1 = c_2$

In the heterogeneous case the effects of abstention may be the opposite of those in the homogeneous case. Table 4-2 illustrates the expanded decision problem.

Recall that for a maximizer the expected value of voting with the stronger group minus the expected value of voting with the weaker group is $c(S_1 - S_2) > 0$. Thus, a maximizer faced with the decision of Table 4-2 never votes against the stronger group.[a] But he may abstain. If $E(a_1) - E(a_2) =$

---

[a]Of course, if the groups are perceived as exactly equal in strength ($S_1 = S_2$), there is no stronger group. In this case a maximizer is indifferent between his two strategies.

Table 4-2
Voting Decisions for a Heterogeneous Constituency, Three-Strategy Case

Probability State / Strategy		$G_1 G_2$ $c_1 c_2$	$G_1 \sim G_2$ $c_1(1 - c_2)$	$\sim G_1 G_2$ $(1 - c_1)c_2$	$\sim G_1 \sim G_2$ $(1 - c)(1 - c_2)$
a_1 with G_1	$x_1 - z_2$	x_1	$-z_2$	0
a_2 abstain	$-y_1 - y_2$	$-y_1$	$-y_2$	0
a_3 against G_1	$-z_1 + x_2$	$-z_1$	x_2	0

$c(x_1 - z_2 + y_1 + y_2) < 0$, then the expected value of voting with the stronger group is less than the expected value of abstaining. So, in touchy situations, maximizers might decide to abstain depending on their estimates of x_1, z_2, y_1, y_2. Note, however, that $E(a_2)$ is always negative. Thus, even though abstention is the optimal strategy in some cases, the maximizer is only making the best of a bad scene. In game theoretic terms, his strategy is minimax: it yields an expectation of the best of the worst. Of course, in all cases in which $E(a_1) > E(a_2)$, the maximizer never abstains; he votes with the stronger group. Given the preceding remarks and the fact that maximizers from homogeneous districts never abstain, we draw another conclusion: given like numbers of votes on which $c_j > 0$, $\forall G_j$, maximizers from heterogeneous constituencies abstain as frequently or more frequently than maximizers from homogeneous constituencies.

For the maintainer the calculation of Q_A is perfectly straightforward.

$$E(\Delta p) = 0 = Q_A c x_1 - Q_A c z_2 - A c y_1 - A c y_2 + (1 - Q_A - A)(-cz_1)$$

$$+ (1 - Q_A - A)(cx_2)$$

$$\frac{z_1 - x_2 + A(y_1 + y_2 + x_2 - z_1)}{x_1 - z_2 + z_1 - x_2} = Q_A \tag{4.3}$$

If $A = 0$, (4.3) reduces to (3.3). Note, however, that unlike the homogeneous case, if $A > 0$, the term $A(y_1 + y_2 + x_2 - z_1)$ is not less than zero in all cases. Rather, it may be greater than, equal to, or less than zero. And, when $A(y_1 + y_2 + x_2 - z_1) > 0$, then $Q_A > Q$. That is, sometimes a maintainer has *less* voting freedom if he assigns some nonzero probability to his abstention strategy than if he does not consider abstention an admissible strategy. When does such a result occur? Most obviously, $Q_A > Q$ if $y_1 = z_1$. Thus, when the stronger constituency group displays a "with us or against us" attitude, a maintainer is more closely bound to the stronger group if he assigns non-zero probability to a_2 than if he does not. Naturally, Q_A may also be greater than Q if y_1 is nearly as large as z_1; i.e., $y_1 > z_1 - y_2 - x_2$, or if y_2 is large. At least one conclusion of substantive interest follows from the preceding facts: In the heterogeneous two-group $c_1 = c_2$ case where a maintaining strategy exists, if members of the stronger constituency group regard an abstention as seriously as an against vote; i.e., $y_1 = z_1$, a maintainer must choose a higher Q if he abstains on some votes than if he were to eliminate the abstention strategy from the decision problem.

Thus, we have the not-unreasonable hypothesis that where the stronger constituency group looks upon nonsupport as tantamount to opposition, the representative may do worse by refusing to adopt a position than by casting a vote. With the latter option he at least makes one side happy, but he satisfies no one with the former. Whereas a maintainer from a homogeneous constituency can usually choose a lower Q (and certainly no higher a Q) by abstaining on some votes, the maintainer from a heterogeneous constituency may be denied such an attractive option.

Of course there are times when the maintainer from a heterogeneous constituency can profitably abstain. In the case just discussed,

(1) $y_1 + y_2 + x_2 - z_1 > 0$, thus $Q_A > Q$.

But if,

(2) $y_1 + y_2 + x_2 - z_1 = 0$, then $Q_A = Q$.

Thus if condition 2 holds, Q with abstention is the same as Q without. Whether a maintainer ever abstains in this situation depends on nonconstituency factors. Finally, if

(3) $y_1 + y_2 + x_2 - z_1 < 0$, then $Q_A < Q$.

In the latter case a maintainer may find it to his advantage to abstain, depending on the possibility of trading abstentions as opposed to votes, a topic discussed earlier.

As in the homogeneous case, the probability assigned to the abstention strategy is not unrestricted. In the most extreme case, if probability Q is assigned to a_1, and $A = (1 - Q)$ to a_2,

$$A = \frac{x_1 - z_2}{y_1 + y_2 + x_1 - z_2} \tag{4.4}$$

Obviously, in any case where some nonzero probability is assigned to a_3, $A < (x_1 - z_2)/(y_1 + y_2 + x_1 - z_2)$. The upper bound given by (4.4) is analogous to (4.2) for the homogeneous case. The most important implications of this restriction are two. First, where no optimal strategy exists (i.e., $x_1 < z_2$) in the two-strategy $c_1 = c_2$ case, (4.4) implies $A < 0$ or $A > 1$, an absurdity. *In the most difficult situation of the two-strategy case, the possibility of abstention does not assuage the maintainer's woes.*[b] All three of his pure strategies have negative expected values; therefore, $E(\Delta p)$ cannot be maintained at 0. Second, where the maintainer is most restricted in the two-strategy case; i.e., where $x_1 = z_2$ implies $Q = 1.0$, (4.4) implies that $A = 0$. We see, then, that *just as in the homogeneous case, the maintainer cannot use the abstention strategy in precisely those situations in which one might have expected (or the maintainer might have hoped) that it would seriously affect our results.*

To summarize, the incorporation of abstention into the analysis of the conflictual, two-group, $c_1 = c_2$ case leads to no striking modifications of our previous analysis. If condition (3) holds, Q_A may drop below $1/2$. If $S_1 = S_2$, a maximizer might abstain rather than be indifferent between his two strategies, although the expected value of his abstention, like his vote, is negative. Similarly, a maintainer without a maintaining strategy may attempt to minimax his loss by abstaining rather than voting either way. But, although the analysis is slightly modified, the fact that the representative is in trouble remains unchanged. If $S_1 > S_2$ a maximizer may abstain rather than vote with the stronger group if $0 > E(a_2) > E(a_1)$. And finally, note that if $c_1 = c_2 > 0$, the c_i are theoretically irrelevant, abstention or not. This conclusion, too, is unaffected by the extension of the theory.

3. Abstention in the General Heterogeneous Two-Group Case

Referring to Table 4-2, we now assume that $c_1 \neq c_2$. For a maximizer the expected values of his strategies are as follows:

$$E(a_1) = c_1 x_1 - c_2 z_2$$

$$E(a_2) = -c_1 y_1 - c_2 y_2$$

$$E(a_3) = -c_1 z_1 + c_2 x_2$$

A maximizer will vote rather than abstain if either of $E(a_1)$, $E(a_3) > E(a_2)$. If $E(a_1) > E(a_3)$, he votes for the stronger group rather than abstain if $E(a_1)$ also exceeds $E(a_2)$, which implies

$$c_1/c_2 > \frac{z_2 - y_2}{x_1 + y_1} \tag{4.5}$$

---

[b]Like the maximizer, the maintainer may find sometimes that abstention is the minimax strategy for a particular decision problem. But this does not alter the fact that no maintaining strategy exists; it only provides a way for him to minimize his losses, providing he chooses to do so.

Note that if $y_2 = z_2$, (4.5) always is satisfied, because c_1, $c_2 > 0$. Thus, in the two-group conflictual case, if the *weaker* group has an "If you're not with us, you're against us" orientation ($y_2 = z_2$), and if $c_1/c_2 > S_2/S_1$, a maximizer votes with the stronger group rather than abstain.

In similar fashion, if $E(a_3) > E(a_1)$, a maximizer will vote for the weaker group if he votes, and he will vote if $E(a_3) > E(a_2)$, or

$$\frac{c_2}{c_1} > \frac{z_1 - y_1}{x_2 + y_2} \tag{4.6}$$

As before, if $y_1 = z_1$, (4.6) is always satisfied since c_1, $c_2 > 0$. Thus, (4.6) yields a conclusion parallel to that yielded by (4.5): in the two-group conflictual case, if the *stronger* group has an "If you're not with us, you're against us" orientation ($y_1 = z_1$), and if $c_1/c_2 < S_2/S_1$, a maximizer votes with the weaker group rather than abstain.

Thus, when considering abstention in the general two-group case, one must examine inequalities (3.5), (3.6), (4.5), and (4.6) in conjunction to predict a maximizer's vote, rather than rely on (3.5) and (3.6) alone. Additionally, recall that if abstention is the most preferred strategy, all strategies have negative expected value. In no case can a maximizer improve on his prevote situation by abstaining. He can only use abstention to minimize the damage he incurs.

Turning now to the maintainer's decision in the general two-group case, we solve for the maintaining strategy as before.

$$\frac{c_1 z_1 - c_2 x_2 + A(c_1 y_1 + c_2 y_2 - c_1 z_1 + c_2 x_2)}{c_1 x_1 - c_2 z_2 + c_1 z_1 - c_2 x_2} = Q_A \tag{4.7}$$

Evidently, if the new term in the numerator of (4.7) is nonzero, our previous conclusions that $Q > .5$, given a Type I maintaining strategy, and $Q < .5$, given a Type II maintaining strategy, may no longer hold. The Q_A given by (4.7) may be greater than, equal to, or less than the Q given by (3.7). In particular, if A is nonzero and

(1') $c_1 y_1 + c_2 y_2 + c_2 x_2 > c_1 z_1$, then $Q_A > Q$

(2') $c_1 y_1 + c_2 y_2 + c_2 x_2 = c_1 z_1$, then $Q_A = Q$

(3') $c_1 y_1 + c_2 y_2 + c_2 x_2 < c_1 z_1$, then $Q_A < Q$

If (1') holds we would expect maintainers to look with displeasure on the abstention strategy. Rather, if a maintaining strategy exists, they would more likely behave in accord with the analysis in Chapter 3. If condition (2') or (3') holds, a maintainer may abstain with some positive probability, or may not, depending on vote-trading possibilities.

Conditions (1'), (2'), (3') are not easy to interpret. We can suggest instances in which these conditions are likely to hold, but the discussion is heuristic, certainly not exhaustive. If c_1 is small, then the likelihood that (1') holds is higher than when c_1 is larger.[c] Conversely, if c_1 is large, the likelihood that (3') holds increases. What we have then is another counterintuitive hypothesis; because a high c_1 makes it more likely that $Q_A < Q$. The minimum probability that the maintainer must vote with the stronger group is likely to be lower when his estimate that the stronger group cares is high than when it is low. Similarly, if c_2 is small, then the likelihood that (3') holds is greater than when c_2 is larger. Conversely, if c_2 is large, the likelihood that (1') holds is greater than when c_2 is small. Thus, a high c_2 makes it more likely that $Q_A > Q$. Because maintainers value flexibility (i.e., a low Q), they are unlikely to abstain with any probability when $Q_A > Q$.

Thus, we see that as the maintainer increases his estimate, c_1, that the stronger group cares, (1) the minimum probability that he must vote with the stronger group decreases in the two-strategy case, (2) the possibility of abstention may lessen the probability he must vote with the stronger group in the three-strategy case. If one is a member of the stronger group, taking actions which cause a maintaining representative to raise c_1 leads either to a decrease in Q or a raise in the likelihood that $Q_A < Q$ depending on whether $A = 0$, or $A > 0$ for the representative.[d] In contrast, as a maintainer increases his estimate, c_2, that the weaker group cares, (1) the minimum probability he must vote with the stronger group increases in the two-strategy case, (2) the likelihood that he will abstain rather than simply vote against the weaker group lessens in the three-strategy case. Members of the weaker group who act so as to cause the maintainer to raise c_2 either cause Q to increase, or raise the likelihood that all residual probability $(1 - Q)$ goes into votes against their group, and not into abstentions, depending on whether $A = 0$, or $A > 0$. Thus, the conclusions of this section reinforce our earlier conclusions about the effects of variations in the c_i on the maintainer's choice of strategy.

Interestingly, if we take partial derivatives of the expected values of the three voting strategies, we find that the likelihood the *maximizer* abstains lessens as c_1 increases and as c_2 increases:

$$\partial E(a_1)/\partial c_1 \geqslant 0, \qquad \partial E(a_2)/\partial c_1 < 0, \qquad \partial E(a_3)/\partial c_1 < 0$$

---

[c]This discussion is an intuitive rendering of the implications of the partial derivatives of (2') with respect to c_1 and c_2, respectively. $\partial(2')/\partial c_1 = (y_1 - z_1) \leqslant 0$. $\partial(2')/\partial c_2 = (y_2 + x_2) > 0$.

[d]The two effects, in general, do not hold simultaneously, however. In the three-strategy case, $\partial Q/\partial c_1$ may be positive, negative, or zero, and similarly for $\partial Q/\partial c_2$. The indeterminacy stems from the fact that we have made no assumption about the relationship of the new variable, y_i, to the old variables, x_i. Thus it proves impossible to evaluate the magnitudes of some of the terms in the partial derivatives.

$$\partial E(a_1)/\partial c_2 < 0, \qquad \partial E(a_2)/\partial c_2 < 0, \qquad \partial E(a_3)/\partial c_2 \geqslant 0$$

From these two sets of partial derivatives, one expects that as the estimate that either group cares increases, the likelihood that a maximizer abstains rather than votes decreases. Specifically, as c_1 increases, the likelihood the maximizer votes with the stronger group increases, while as c_2 increases, the likelihood he votes with the weaker group increases. So we see that the variables c_1, c_2, exert an opposite influence on the voting of maximizers and maintainers in both two- and three-strategy cases.

Finally, observe that (4.8) expresses the maximum probability that a maintainer can assign to his abstention strategy given the existence of a Type I maintaining strategy, while (4.9) is the analogous expression given existence of a Type II maintaining strategy.

$$A = \frac{c_1 x_1 - c_2 z_2}{c_1 y_1 + c_2 y_2 + c_1 x_1 - c_2 z_2} \tag{4.8}$$

$$A = \frac{-c_1 z_1 + c_2 x_2}{c_1 y_1 + c_2 y_2 - c_1 z_1 + c_2 x_2} \tag{4.9}$$

Evidently, (4.2) and (4.4) are special cases of (4.8). Most importantly, note that the numerators of (4.8) and (4.9) contain the terms expressing the necessary and sufficient conditions for the existence of Type I and Type II maintaining strategies, respectively. If neither a Type I nor a Type II strategy exists; i.e., $c_1 x_1 < c_2 z_2$ and $c_1 z_1 > c_2 x_2$, A will be greater than one or less than zero, an absurdity. In this situation a maintainer might abstain if that action entails the minimum loss, but as in the $c_1 = c_2$ case, abstention does not affect the existence of a maintaining strategy.

In summary, we have the following conclusions about abstention in the two-group conflictual constituency.

1. Both maximizers and maintainers may abstain as a loss-minimization strategy. Additionally, under some conditions, maintainers can lower Q_A by assigning some probability to their abstention strategy.
2. Because maximizers from consensual districts never abstain, all representatives from conflictual districts should have abstention rates at least as high as maximizers from consensual districts on votes for which $c_i > 0$.
3. Both maximizers and maintainers are less likely to abstain on votes which arouse a "He who is not with me is against me" reaction ($y_i = z_i$) among constituents.
4. Abstention does not change the conditions under which maintaining strategies exist in the two-strategy case.
5. Abstention does not increase a maintainer's flexibility in those situations in

which he is bound ($Q = 1$) to a constituency group in the two-strategy case.

6. As the probability that either group cares increases, the likelihood that a maximizer abstains decreases. For maintainers the situation differs. As the probability the stronger group cares increases, the likelihood that $Q_A < Q$ increases; i.e., the possibility of abstention becomes more attractive. As the probability the weaker group cares increases, the likelihood that $Q_A > Q$ increases, suggesting that a maintainer will not abstain with any probability.

This completes our consideration of abstention as a voting strategy. While we have uncovered a number of logical implications, none suggest drastic revision of the earlier analysis. Abstention modifies a few propositions made previously; e.g., ($Q > .5$), but specifications of overall tendencies and identifications of tough decisions are unaffected by the theoretical availability of the abstention option. Thus, the discussion of abstention might be described as a tangent off the basic model, although an interesting tangent. Probably the major importance of the abstention analysis is its potential for empirical testing. We have learned that in the model, maximizers from consensual districts will have lower abstention votes than all other representatives. In Chapter 5 we will examine this prediction in the light of some congressional data.

The N-Group Constituency

Thus far we have focused almost exclusively on voting decisions given one or two groups with nonzero c_j. But in Chapter 3 we commented that conclusions about voting decisions with a consensual constituency extend unchanged from two-group to N-group decisions. Similarly, with a conflictual constituency we noted that the dependence of Q on the c_i changes as we proceed from two to more than two groups. Thus, we have examined the N-group situations, although we have not discussed them at length.

Basically, we are not terribly confident in the empirical accuracy of our N-group formulations, at least less so than in the one- and two-group formulations. The analysis thus far has employed an additivity assumption. Specifically, $S_{(1,2)} = S_1 + S_2 = (x_1 + x_2 + z_1 + z_2)$. That is, we have assumed that group strength is additive. Using this assumption, the one- and two-group analysis extends easily to N-groups. One speaks of stronger and weaker *sets* of groups, naturally, but conclusions about Q being greater or less than .5, equal c_j, conditions for existence of maintaining strategies, etc., are exactly analogous to those in the two-group case. On the other hand, propositions about the dependence of Q on various c_i, x_i, z_i do not extend. These relationships are indeterminate.

The problem is the additivity assumption. An analogy due to Arthur

Goldberg perfectly illustrates the question involved.[2] Imagine a man attempting to dodge a snowball thrown by another man. There is a nonzero probability, p, of a hit. Now a second snowball thrower appears on the scene. If both throw simultaneously, presumably the target is more likely to be hit than in the one-thrower situation, perhaps with probability, $2p$. A third thrower appears. Is the probability of a hit now $3p$, or is it greater? As more and more throwers enter the contest, the probability of a hit becomes almost certain. The target has the nearly hopeless task of dodging numerous snowballs thrown at once. Additivity of probabilities simply does not describe the situation accurately. And probably, the more numerous the throwers, the less accurate is the additivity assumption. This is our problem in a nutshell. Perhaps additivity is reasonable when two opposing groups care about the issue. But what if seven groups feel one way and two the other? How do we calculate the strength of the seven-group side? In all likelihood it is more than the sum of the individual strengths.

What may be needed is a richer theory of coalition dynamics. Such a theory could be embedded in a theory of constituency influence. Existing coalition theories are not adequate to the task. They typically focus on divisions of payoffs, sizes of coalitions, and makeup of coalitions given well-specified criteria for winning in elite arenas.[3] But we need to know more accurately how coalitions utilize numbers and other resources, how they mobilize members, and how they augment their strength by combining with other coalitions in mass arenas characterized by great uncertainty. Perhaps coalition isn't even the correct term. Possibly we need a new group theory more so than a richer coalition theory.

Just how serious is the lack of a model which accurately characterizes roll-call voting decisions with N-group constituency configurations? Well, the writings of legislative scholars abound in familiar dichotomies: Republican-Democrat, urban-rural, white-black, Catholic-Protestant, labor-business. Perhaps we can get by for a time on models which presume at most two contending groups. Perhaps the great uncertainty about constituency preferences prevents a representative from differentiating more finely than pro-anti.[e] Perhaps on many decisions only one group has a nonzero c. Our general impression from the literature is that each of these "perhaps" is more accurate than not, but they raise empirical questions which only can be answered empirically.

The M-Issue Voting Decision

In commenting on the basic model, theoretically inclined colleagues have been nearly unanimous in focusing on the limited time horizon presumed. Our model of the voting decision treats each vote as if it were the last. The representative is

---

[e]This would imply that representatives view their constituencies more in terms of issue publics than in terms of the more traditional socioeconomic categories.

assumed to vote (at least attempt to vote) in such a way that at all times he is as strong electorally as he would like to be for the next campaign. In effect, there is no tomorrow in the model. To some, such a formulation is unsatisfactory. Why can't a representative vote against constituents at the beginning of a session and make it up later? Why not have a representative formulate a maximizing or maintaining strategy over all the votes in a session? If there were M votes in a session, an optimal strategy could take the form of an M-tuple of $1, 0, -1$ values (pro, abstain, con). In this way a maintainer at least could pick and choose the votes on which he would follow district preferences. Additionally, the theoretically convenient but empirically troublesome concept of probabilistic choice (i.e., mixed strategies) largely could be avoided. Is the extension of the model to M-issue decisions a highly desirable undertaking, then? In our opinion, no.

The basic problem with an M-issue decision model is that it has nothing to do with the empirical world. Sometimes theorists generalize results for no other reason than that generalizing is widely considered to be a good thing to do. One can easily generalize a model into irrelevancy. Let us consider a few facts about American legislative bodies, the Congress in particular, facts which make doubtful the applicability of an M-issue decision model.

An M-issue model assumes that a representative looks ahead to see what proposals he will be voting on during the coming session. To what extent can this assumption hold? Well, if a representative is so inclined, he can keep tabs on bills and resolutions introduced in his house and in the other body. But, then what? Any freshman student knows that funny things happen on the way to the floor. Will the proposal clear subcommittee? Will it clear the full committee? Will it clear the Rules Committee (in the House) or escape filibuster (in the Senate)? When? Will it be lost in the end-of-session rush or buried by unsympathetic floor leaders? Moreover, in what form will the proposal reach the floor? What will the subcommittee, full committee, Rules Committee, other house or Conference Committee do to it? What debilitating amendments will the proposal's enemies offer? What began as a moderate, labor-supported, labor reform bill eventually emerged as Landrum-Griffin in 1959.[4] What would this have done to an optimal M-issue voting strategy calculated previously?

When legislative scholars write of the congressional labyrinth or the obstacle course on Capitol Hill, they aren't simply engaging in hyperbole.[5] They are characterizing the features of the legislative process which make M-issue voting strategies impossible. Rank and file legislators complain that they often don't know what's going on.[6] Party leaders announce the agenda a week in advance, if that. Procedural coups keep bills off the floor, and unforeseen amendments force the making of unexpected decisions. Typically, a representative answers the signal for a roll call unaware of precisely what he is going to the floor to vote on. Facts like these have led a number of legislative scholars to abandon decision theoretic models altogether, let alone M-issue models.[7] Empirically, the uncertainties of the legislative process force representatives to operate in the short term. They simply do not possess the information to formulate long-term strategies.

At the risk of overkill, we will make another point. Elected officials appear to be risk-averse in general. The word "politician" has come to signify someone without convictions, who leans with each momentary breeze. Yet the *M*-issue decision model presumes that a representative votes against someone *now* on the assumption that he can make it up *later*. This presupposes considerable courage on the part of politicians—foolish courage in view of the nature of the legislative process. And politicians are not fools. Representatives treat each vote as if it might be the last precisely because it could be.

To sum up, then, we would argue against any attempt to utilize long-term models for roll-call voting decisions, unless plausible short-term models are conclusively rejected. Our present model includes the past, but not the future.[f] And we are convinced that this is the proper state of affairs.

Some Thoughts on Payoffs and State Probabilities

The concepts of group strength, S_j, and group concern, c_j, have played an important role in our analysis. When these concepts were introduced in Chapter 2, we remarked that the model takes these estimates as givens, although ideally a more complete model of constituency influence would account for them. In this section we will set out a few preliminary ideas about the process by which a representative might estimate the strength and concern parameters for his voting decision problem.

First, consider group strength. When we think of political strength, we naturally think first of votes. Votes are the currency of electoral politics. Of course, resources other than votes also affect judgments of group strength. Such obvious resources as money and manpower clearly loom large in the eyes of political decision makers. Yet at some level, all resources eventually translate into votes; hence, their value. This series of relationships lends itself to translation as a system of equations.

For our purposes the most basic political characteristic of a group is size, denoted by n, the number of members. The number of voting members, v, is a function of size and institutional considerations, I_1, (for example, laws regulating the right to vote). Formally,

---

[f]To elaborate, a cardinal tenet of the subjectivist school asserts the conditional nature of all probabilities. There are no a priori probabilities; every probability is conditional upon the circumstances surrounding it. From the standpoint of our model, this means that the probability estimates in the decision problem for the mth vote reflect the consequences of the preceding ($m - 1$) votes, as well as any new information which comes to the representative's attention. (The estimates for a vote on a minimum wage bill which occurs at the beginning of a session need not be the same as the estimates for the same bill later in the session.) Thus, the theory does include the effects of preceding actions on current decisions, the past, if not the future.

$$v = f^1 (n, I_1),\qquad\qquad (4.10)$$

where n and I_1 are themselves functions of variables outside the model.[g]

i.e., $n = \phi(\alpha_1, \ldots, \alpha_n)$ $I_1 = \psi(B_1, \ldots, B_n)$.

We signify the monetary resources available to a group as m. Presumably m will vary with group size and also with exogenous variables $\gamma_1, \ldots, \gamma_m$ such as economic characteristics of the group members:

$$m = f^2 (n, \gamma_1, \ldots, \gamma_n)\qquad\qquad (4.11)$$

Additionally, m might depend on institutional constraints, I_2, such as campaign finance laws.

The amount of time available from group campaign workers, w, again will depend on the size of the group along with exogenous variables $\delta_1, \ldots, \delta_n$, such as the occupations, age, and marital status of group members:

$$w = f^3 (n, \delta_1, \ldots, \delta_n)\qquad\qquad (4.12)$$

Then we may postulate that group strength is a function of the votes, money, and workers a group can provide:

$$x = g^1 (v, m, w)$$

$$z = g^2 (v, m, w)\qquad\qquad (4.13)$$

$$S = x + z$$

These functions must be constrained to yield meaningful probability numbers, and, in the case of our model, to yield $z \geqslant x$. Presumably x and z will increase or at least not decline as v, m, and w increase; but we would hesitate to suggest what rate of increase one should expect, or even that a continuous increase should be expected. Note that given (4.10) to (4.12) one can substitute in (4.13) to express group strength as some function of group size, institutional restrictions, and socioeconomic characteristics of group members, a quite plausible formulation.

Group concern is not quite so straightforward to handle as group strength. The probability that a group reacts to an issue *qua* group depends on several factors, some of them unfortunately imprecise. First, one would expect the

[g]What is and what is not outside the model of course is an arbitrary decision rather than a matter of incontrovertible fact. At this stage we simply assume that some variables are determined outside the model.

degree of organization, o, of a group to count. Additionally, group unity or cohesion, u, will be important. Unity and organization no doubt are related, but each also depends on exogenous factors such as ethnic or cultural ties in the case of cohesion, and communications and commonality of interest in the case of organization. Thus,

$$o = h^1 (u, \tau_1, \ldots, \tau_n) \qquad (4.14)$$

$$u = h^2 (o, \sigma_1, \ldots, \sigma_n) \qquad (4.15)$$

And, certainly, the intensity of preference, i, of group members affects c. We are fully aware of the difficulties and ambiguities surrounding the concept of intensity. But despite the failure of social scientists to produce a clear formulation of intensity, few doubt that it exists and that it matters. In sum,

$$c = l^1 (o, u, i) \qquad (4.16)$$

where intensity remains a basic given for the present time.

A modification of (4.16) that we might wish to consider is (4.16)′,

$$c = l^2 (o, u, i, r) \qquad (4.16)′$$

where r is a representative's past voting record. Perhaps a group does have some concern for an issue if considered in isolation. But if a representative has gone down the line for them on a series of much more crucial votes, they might have a zero probability of turning against him on the basis of the issue at hand. Similarly, if he has opposed them previously, a not terribly important issue could be the straw that breaks the camel's back. Making c a function of r admits these kinds of reactions.

In the present basic model we have assumed that estimates of c and S are independent. The preceding formulations ((4.10) to (4.16)′) allow the independence assumption to hold. But how might it go wrong? Two possibilities appear most likely.

First, it may be that representatives do not just discount group strength by the probability of group concern as in our model, but rather that they include that probability as part of the estimate of group strength. Thus (4.13) might be modified to (4.13)′:

$$x = g^3 (v, m, w, c)$$
$$\qquad\qquad\qquad\qquad (4.13)′$$
$$z = g^4 (v, m, w, c)$$

Empirically, when we think of politically strong groups we tend to include their willingness to act politically as part of their strength. Whether this is only sloppy thinking on our part or a fundamental property of strength as in (4.13)$'$ remains to be seen.

The independence assumption also could fail in a second way: if c and S are both functions of some one or more common variables. For example, Olson has argued that the likelihood of effective action by a group relates inversely to group size.[8] The larger the group, the less organized and cohesive it will be, and the less likely will it be to act effectively. Thus, (4.14), (4.15) and (4.16) are modified to

$$o = h^3 (u,n,\tau_1, \ldots, \tau_n) \tag{4.14$'$}$$

$$u = h^4 (o,n,\sigma_1, \ldots, \sigma_n) \tag{4.15$'$}$$

$$c = l^3 (o,u,i,n) \tag{4.16$'$}$$

Now S and c are both functions of at least one common factor, group size, and clearly not independent. Of course, in the early 1970s we are seeing frequent political efforts by large public interest groups such as environmental and consumer organizations. So, perhaps past tendencies for smaller special interest groups to dominate political activity were more a coincidence than a pervasive feature of political reality.

Enough has been written in this section to indicate the dimensions of the problem we face, and why we began by taking estimates of S and c as givens. The questions raised will be topics of future research for a rather lengthy future. Isolating the major variables affecting group strength and concern should not be terribly difficult. But theorizing about the relationships among them and carrying out the measurements necessary for empirical estimation pose no easy task. Yet if the S_j and c_j are important variables in a representative's voting decision problem, then eventually we must face up to these problems.

Notes

1. Congressional Quarterly Voting Participation and On the Record Scores, drawn from the annual *Congressional Quarterly Almanacs*.

2. Arthur Goldberg, "A Theoretical Approach to Political Stability," APSA Paper, Washington, D.C., 1968, p. 6.

3. See, for example, William Riker, *The Theory of Political Coalitions* (New Haven: Yale, 1962). Sven Groennings, E.W. Kelley and Michael Leiserson, *The Study of Coalition Behavior* (New York: Holt, Rinehart and Winston, 1970). Robert Axelrod, *Conflict of Interest* (Chicago: Markham, 1970), Chapter 8.

4. Samuel Patterson, *Labor Lobbying and Labor Reform* (Indianapolis: Bobbs-Merrill, 1966).

5. Robert Bendiner, *Obstacle Course on Capitol Hill* (New York: McGraw-Hill, 1946). Nelson Polsby, "The Labyrinth: A Bill Becomes a Law," in *Congress and the Presidency* (Englewood Cliffs: Prentice-Hall, 1964), pp. 62-81.

6. For example, see the criticisms of the House leadership in Clapp, *The Congressman: His Work As He Sees It*, pp. 329-332.

7. See in particular the recently advanced "cue-taking" models. Donald Matthews and James Stimson, "Decision-Making by U.S. Representatives: A Preliminary Model," in S. Sidney Ulmer (ed.), *Political Decision-Making* (New York: Van Nostrand Reinhold Company, 1970), pp. 14-43. Cleo Cherryholmes and Michael Shapiro, *Representatives and Roll Calls: A Computer Simulation of Voting in the Eighty-Eighth Congress* (Indianapolis: Bobbs-Merrill, 1968).

8. Mancur Olson, *The Logic of Collective Action* (New York: Schocken, 1968).

5

Some Preliminary Empirical Applications

Introduction

Until applied, models are merely sets of logical relationships—castles in the air. Regrettably, theorists often fail to bridge the gap between logical and empirical, a failure which probably has lowered political scientists' esteem for the theoretical enterprise. What accounts for the gulf between theoretical and empirical work in Political Science? Two factors appear paramount.

First, the data demands of some models clearly exceed existing empirical measurement technology. For example, recent years have seen the development of models "testable in principle, but not in practice." These models rest on the assumption of expected utility maximization, and techniques for measuring utility outside simple laboratory situations just do not exist. But while empirical researchers may be less than enthusiastic about theories not as yet testable, they are not thereby justified in rejecting such theories. Rather, one should remember that the history of science frequently shows measurement technologies developing in order to keep pace with advancing theories. A theory "testable in principle" should be viewed as a challenge, not rejected because of empirical limitations. Perhaps the present relatively primitive state of conceptualization and measurement in Political Science stems from our collective failure to propose theories which went beyond everyday vagaries. Had we been more daring in theory construction in past years, "testable in practice" might now encompass a greater capability than it does.

A second reason a theory may not be tested is simply lack of interest. The theorist himself does not attempt to test the theory, and it fails to catch the fancy of any empirical workers. While unfortunate, this situation perhaps is unavoidable. A theorist incurs no moral duty to test his formulations. Like other complex activities, science is characterized by a division of labor. Some researchers enjoy building model worlds, some enjoy collecting and analyzing data. One cannot say that a good theorist will make a good data analyst, or vice-versa.

We believe that the model advanced in Chapters 2, 3, and 4 is testable in practice as well as in principle. Admittedly, the data may be difficult to gather—so far as we know legislators have never been asked to make numerous subjective probability estimates. This is not to say that they cannot, however. A full-scale test of the theory will necessitate living with representatives in their natural habitat for an extended period. But although unable to carry out such an extensive test at present, we have elected to perform several preliminary indirect tests of the theoretical implications. In the applications to follow, we have made various auxiliary assumptions to relate theoretical variables to available data. The difficulty with such indirect tests, of course, inheres in the question of attributing disconfirming instances to an erroneous theory or erroneous auxiliary assumptions. In the face of contrary data the theorist can always reject the test; in Northrup's terms, the process of epistemic correlation went awry.[1] And in similar fashion, in the face of confirming data the skeptical critic can suggest that both theory and auxiliary assumptions were incorrect. In some cases two wrongs do make a right.

In addition to testing hypotheses based on theoretical relationships one also can ask what the theory does to organize and explicate existing knowledge. Does the theory connect the seemingly disparate findings of other studies? Does it provide a rationale for the surprising findings of an atheoretical study? Does it reconcile apparent contradictions? These are all in a sense indirect tests of a theory. In fact, the theory which does the preceding, even if not directly testable, may be more valuable than the directly testable theory which accomplishes none of the preceding.

Safe-Marginal or
Homogeneous-Heterogeneous?

In developing a model of constituency influence we classified constituencies as consensual or conflictual with respect to a given vote. If a representative estimates that $c_{jk} > 0$ for only one group, or only for groups who would agree upon how he should vote, we call his constituency consensual or homogeneous with respect to the issue k. Alternatively, if $c_{jk} > 0$ for more than one group, some of whom would disagree, we call the constituency conflictual or heterogeneous.[a] We have argued that this classification scheme underlies a more familiar one: safe-competitive. That is, districts which political scientists classify as safe are those which tend to be homogeneous on most votes, while marginal districts tend to be heterogeneous. The relationship between the two classification schemes is important for two reasons. First, it constitutes a link between the implications of our model and much of the existing literature on constituency and roll call voting. Second, because our theory predicts a correspondence of homogeneity-heterogeneity to safe-marginal; the existence of that correspondence would offer some corroboration for the theory.

Note that on theoretical grounds we claim that homogeneity-heterogeneity is a more fundamental dimension than safe-marginal. In consensual constituencies profitable (at least not harmful) voting strategies always exist. Thus, in districts

---

[a] If $c_j = 0$ for all groups, the representative has no constituency with respect to the issue under consideration. See Chapter 2.

which usually can be symbolized by the homogeneous configuration, a representative can raise or maintain his subjective probability of reelection by voting in an optimal fashion, i.e., he can make himself safe. Conversely, in heterogeneous districts, profitable strategies do not always exist. Thus, in districts which typically must be symbolized by a heterogeneous configuration, a representative may frequently see his subjective probability of reelection fall, no matter how he votes. Unless district homogeneity relates positively to district safety, the preceding chain of logic is wrong. In this section we will demonstrate the existence of this relationship. Three modes of argument are employed: first, appeals to the self-evidence of the relationship; second, appeals to authority; and third and most important, appeals to data.

Consider the nature of the tradtionally defined safe areas in the United States. On the national level, the prototype is the rural, agrarian, Protestant, Southern Democratic district. Until the late 1960s, blacks—the major source of heterogeneity in such districts—were legally and socially proscribed from the political arena. The prospect of increasing electoral competition in such areas is associated closely with increasing heterogeneity, the latter resulting from black voter registration. The rural Republican areas of the Midwest and Northeast include other traditionally safe districts. Are not such areas relatively homogeneous? Writing in the early 1960s, J.M. Burns described safe districts as " . . . made up of villages, small towns, and small cities. They have a heavily rural bias. Compared to the larger metropolitan areas, these districts tend to be more homogeneous in social make-up and political attitude."[2] And, according to various authors, small-town America gives free rein to pressures for conformity, or, in our terms, homogeneity.[3] In recent years we have seen new Democratic strongholds rise in the poor, black, rather homogeneous cores of our cities. Interestingly, in the 1950s, Huntington and later Eulau argued that increasing urbanization with accompanying increasing diversity of interests (heterogeneity) would lead to increasing party competition in the United States.[4] They could not foresee the eventual division of heterogeneous metropolitan areas into relatively homogeneous subareas of core city and suburb.

Obviously, the concept of competition implies heterogeneity. In a marginal district disagreement exists; two or more groups are in opposition on some dimensions. Indeed, were we willing to assume that all constituency divisions are party divisions, our argument might well end here. For to class a district as competitive is to assert tautologically that the district is heterogeneous along a party preference dimension. Were we willing to presume the primacy of party conflicts, the degree of party competition would be the obvious operational definition of district heterogeneity. But we are wary of reducing all constituency divisions to party divisions. Some conflicts of interest cut across party lines. Urban-rural, and regional conflicts are examples. Additionally, some conflicts split the parties. Within the Republican party, big and small business may not see eye-to-eye. "Radical" intellectuals may rail at "reactionary" labor within the

Democratic party. Thus, by letting any and all group conflicts define heterogeneity, rather than just party conflict, we retain a more general theory.

Still, one cannot deny that party frequently serves as an umbrella under which other divisions gather. The parties compete along different dimensions in different constituencies. Party competition might mask urban-rural conflict in some districts, business-labor in others, and black-white in still others. But one would be forced to admit that the general variable of party competition measures some source of district heterogeneity in each case, although the measurement may be highly imperfect and the sources of heterogeneity quite different. Thus, we would continue to regard safe-competitive as an important classification. But we believe that its importance stems from its rough correspondence to a more basic dimension: homogeneous-heterogeneous. District competition is a derivative variable, one which largely reflects the underlying configuration of the district. Only if the distribution of constituency preferences is heterogeneous along some salient dimension, will a district be competitive. Only if dimensions on which preferences are heterogeneous are kept out of the political arena, will a district be safe.

Certainly, we are not original in arguing for a relationship between district homogeneity on the one hand and electoral competition on the other. The argument is something of a commonplace observation in the writings of legislative scholars. A sampling of their statements is illustrative.

In the first place, of course, it is the diversity in part that creates the atmosphere for two-party competition, and the absence of diversity facilitates one-partyism. (Lockard)[5]

... the same factors that render a district safe for one party or the other may also make it easier to represent. That is, one-party areas tend to be more homogeneous in population and political interests than competitive areas. (Davidson)[6]

... competitive districts with mixed socio-economic characteristics tend to produce "moderate" legislators in both parties, while noncompetitive districts with dominant socio-economic characteristics tend to produce "liberal" Democrats and "conservative" Republicans. (Keefe)[7]

Decisive winners and losers, first of all, believe more than marginal candidates do that there is some group in their district which they must keep satisfied in order to win. . . . Decisive districts then, are apparently rather homogeneous and tend to be dominated by a single group of people that candidates feel they need to satisfy, more than are marginal districts. (Kingdon)[8]

... lack of competitiveness is a sign of greater homogeneity of constituency factors within the district. (Froman)[9]

And, consider Huntington's extended remarks,

In any rural area there is usually only one dominant economic interest. Whether this be cotton, corn, wheat, or dairy farming, the economic life of the area is dependent upon that one interest. Consequently both parties in that area reflect that interest. Since, therefore, there are no real differences between the parties the choice of party is determined by non-economic historical and traditional factors. Once this choice has been determined by historical circumstance, there are no conflicts of economic interest to cause it to be altered; the candidates of the same party are continually returned to office; and thus there arises a perpetually dominant party. This is generally the Republican party in the rural North and the Democratic party in the rural South. In these areas the second major party loses its most important characteristic, its monopoly of opposition. In the first place, there is no basic opposition for it to express, and secondly, those personality differences and differences on minor issues which do arise can be settled in the major party's primaries. It is a well recognized characteristic of rural one-party politics that it tends to be based largely on personalities and to follow a "friends and neighbors" pattern. The second major party hence ceases in a very real sense to be a major party and declines to the status of a minor party. Socially and economically it is composed of the same elements which make up the dominant party; politically its principal importance is as a dispenser of federal patronage. This is true of the Democratic party in northern rural districts and of the Republican party in southern rural districts.

In urban and suburban districts, a different situation exists. Instead of one dominant economic interest there are here two competing economic interests, one composed of middle and upper class property owning, capitalistic groups, the other composed of lower class, propertyless, laboring elements. The economic conflict between these groups is direct and sharp. Within the narrow confines of a single urban area no party could represent them both. Consequently one party tends to adjust itself to represent one interest and the other party accommodates itself to the other interest; one becomes the party of labor and the lower class and the other the party of business and the upper class. Economic conflict and not tradition determines party loyalties. Since these two conflicting economic interests are generally fairly evenly matched in most urban areas, the two parties likewise become evenly balanced. Naturally there are exceptions: in an overwhelmingly slum area the lower class party will prevail. Usually, however, upper and lower classes are found together in a relatively restricted area and hence the parties representing them tend towards numerical equality. (Huntington)[10]

But while we are not original in arguing for a correspondence between the dimensions of safe-marginal and homogeneous-heterogeneous, in considering the latter dimension as fundamental and relegating the former dimension to a subsidiary position, the emphasis of our argument breaks with the traditional view. We do not expect district safety to correlate with voting behavior because the degree of safety is a rough measure of the representative's confidence in his reelection chances. Rather, we expect district safety to correlate with voting behavior because the degree of safety is a rough indicator of the homogeneity or heterogeneity of the constituency.

We now have stated our argument as clearly as possible, supporting it on the grounds of intuitive plausibility, the arguments of fellow legislative scholars, and theoretical facts about the existence of optimal voting strategies. Naturally, and justifiably, however, many researchers will wish to see some actual data on the homogeneity-heterogeneity vs. safe-marginal question. In the remainder of this section we present and discuss such data. Given the theoretical argument we have presented, this data provides a rough test of the entire theoretical structure.

We have performed two separate analyses. The first examines the relationship between the socioeconomic diversity of states and electoral margins in the 1958, 1960, and 1962 elections for U.S. Senator. The second analysis employs survey data from the 1958 SRC representation study. Electoral margins in a nonrandom sample of 58 Congressional districts are related to attitudinal heterogeneity within those districts.

First, the U.S. Senate analysis. Between 1958 and 1962, 110 elections for the office of U.S. Senator occurred. We have taken the winner's proportion of the vote in each of these elections as our dependent variable.[b] As a measure of the primary independent variable of interest we have used John Sullivan's diversity scores for the American states. The scores are based on educational, occupational, income, housing, ethnic, and religious data. Admittedly, socioeconomic diversity may not be a very precise measure of the degree of political cleavage in a state, and a summary measure could lump together unimportant and important variables. Still, Sullivan shows that the calculated diversity scores correlate moderately to strongly with a variety of political and policy measures. Therefore, we will rely on these summary scores for the Senate analysis.

Table 5-1 contains the results of a simple linear regression of Senate winners' proportions on the Sullivan diversity scores.[c] Evidently, the predicted relationship holds. For Mississippi (diversity = .33) one expects the winner of a Senate

Table 5-1
Senate Winners' Proportions as a Function of State Diversity

B	σ_B	R^2	a	s.e.e.
−.73	.18	.14	.93	.11

[b]The 1958, 1960 and 1962 elections were chosen because Sullivan's diversity scores are calculated from the 1960 census. In addition, choice of the six-year period includes at least two elections from each state.

[c]In this section we perform statistical analyses of nonrandom samples: all Senate elections between 1958 and 1962, and 58 House elections chosen on the basis of the r.umber of district citizens interviewed. We assume this nonrandomness does not systematically bias our results. Additionally, the limited dependent variable introduces a heteroskedasticity problem which may affect the tests of significance. At this stage of the research we have chosen not to employ complex techniques to handle this problem. Thus, although we report the standard errors for all estimates and indicate those estimates which do not attain statistical significance using conventional t and F tests ($p < .05$), these figures should be interpreted cautiously.

election to receive 69 percent of the vote. For Washington (diversity = .45) the expected percentage of the victor is 60 percent. And for New York (diversity = .56) the expected winning percentage is 52 percent.

In an attempt to improve the fit of the regression equation and obtain a better estimate of the independent impact of diversity on winning percentage, we added two obvious variables to the analysis.[d] These include an incumbency dummy (incumbent = 1, 0 otherwise) and a South (old Confederacy) dummy (South = 1, 0 otherwise). In addition we have created two variables, southern diversity and nonsouthern diversity, to replace the previous diversity variable. (5.1) is the basic specification.

$$y = a + b_1 D (1 - S) + b_2 S + b_3 I + b_4 (D \cdot S) \qquad (5.1)$$

where y = Senate winner's percentage

D = Sullivan diversity score

S = South dummy, South = 1

I = Incumbency dummy, Incumbent = 1

Substituting dummy values, one gets for non-Southerners

$$y = a + b_1 D + b_3 I \qquad (5.2)$$

while for Southerners one gets

$$y = (a + b_2) + b_3 I + b_4 D \qquad (5.3)$$

In words, (5.1) allows both the intercept and the estimate of the diversity slope to vary between South and non-South. Except for the constraint that the incumbency slope is constant between regions (5.1) is conceptually equivalent to splitting the data set and running separate regressions for each set. But (5.1) permits use of all 110 data points in the estimation rather than subsets of 87 and 23 points. Table 5-2 contains the estimates for (5.1). Evidently, we have managed to cloud the waters as much as clarify. For non-Southerners our prediction is as follows:

$$y = .46 + .19D + .04I$$

For Southerners our prediction is

$$y = 1.02 + .04I - .83D$$

---

[d]Thanks are due to David Grether of Caltech, for his advice on the analysis reported in this section.

Table 5-2

Senate Winners' Proportions as a Function of Diversity, South, and Incumbency

Variable	B	σ_B	R^2	a	s.e.e.
NS. Diversity	.19*	.20			
South	.56	.19			
Incumbency	.04	.02	.46	.46	.09
S. Diversity	−.83	.44			

*not significant.

In the South diversity retains its negative relationship to electoral margins. But in the non-South the estimated slope for diversity is smaller than its standard error and *positive*. An incumbent running in Mississippi (diversity = .33) gets 79 percent of the vote according to our estimates, whereas his counterpart running in more diverse Texas (diversity = .44) gets 69 percent. But in the North an opposite situation holds. An incumbent running in Indiana (diversity = .41) gets 58 percent whereas his counterpart running in more diverse Massachusetts (diversity = .54) gets 60 percent.

Well, what does one conclude? Is diversity related to electoral marginality in the South but not in the rest of the country? Are the variables which constitute the diversity measure better indicators of relevant attitudinal cleavages in the South than in the non-South? Frankly, we don't know. Perhaps the analysis of electoral marginality in the U.S. House of Representatives will clarify matters.

For our second analysis we use data from the 1958 SRC representation study. Our sample of Congressional districts is nonrandom: we have chosen to analyze the 58 districts in which ten or more citizens were interviewed. That is, we selected districts in which the unweighted n equaled or exceeded 10. After choosing the districts for analysis, the data were weighted appropriately. A listing of districts follows in Table 5-3. In three issue areas, Foreign Affairs, Social Welfare, and Civil Rights (FA, SW, CR), respondents' attitudes were Guttman scaled. We have examined the distribution of constituents along each issue dimension in each of the 58 districts. Two measures are employed. First, we have computed the variance (var) of each constituency sample on each of the three dimensions. Because this presumes an interval level measurement, and Guttman scales are ordinal at best, use of the variance is open to question. But given that political scientists habitually treat Guttman scales as interval measures, we will do likewise and present the variance measure, if only for heuristic purposes.

In addition, we have computed an estimate, $\bar{m}$, which represents the proportion of each district sample which occupies the mode of the attitude distribution along each dimension. This measure is more suitable for ordinal and nominal level data, but it is insensitive to the locations of nonmodal constituents.

One would expect $\bar{m}$ and var to have a negative relationship. $\bar{m}$ may be

Table 5-3
Data from the 1958 SRC Representation Study

Non-Southern (*n* = 42)		Southern (*n* = 16)	
State	District	State	District
Connecticut	2	Virginia	9
Connecticut	4	Alabama	2
Massachusetts	4	Arkansas	4
New Jersey	5	Arkansas	5
New York	2	Florida	3
New York	22	Florida	7
New York	31	Georgia	8
New York	35	Georgia	9
New York	36	Louisiana	5
Pennsylvania	7	Mississippi	4
Pennsylvania	10	North Carolina	1
Pennsylvania	11	North Carolina	5
Pennsylvania	21	North Carolina	9
Michigan	4	South Carolina	2
Michigan	6	Texas	17
Michigan	7	Texas	22
Michigan	18		
Ohio	3		
Ohio	17		
Indiana	11		
Wisconsin	9		
Iowa	3		
Iowa	6		
Iowa	7		
Kansas	6		
Minnesota	4		
Minnesota	7		
Nebraska	1		
South Dakota	1		
Colorado	3		
Idaho	1		
New Mexico	AL		
California	8		
California	12		
California	25		
California	28		
California	30		
Washington	6		
Missouri	9		
Kentucky	1		
Kentucky	3		
Kentucky	7		

thought of as an estimate of homogeneity: the larger the proportion of constituents in the same scale position, the more homogeneous is the constituency. Conversely, var can be considered an estimate of heterogeneity: as the variance of the distribution of constituents along the scale increases, heterogeneity increases. Obviously, the $\overline{m}$ measures should have a positive relationship with electoral safety, while the variance measures should have a negative relationship.

As previously, to operationalize the variable, safety, we employ the winner's proportion of the vote. First, then, we estimate the relationship between House winning proportions and the several measures of district attitudinal homogeneity/heterogeneity. Given the three dimensions of the latter and the two intercorrelated measures of each dimension, we have employed a stepwise regression procedure to ascertain the most important (if any) measures of homogeneity/heterogeneity. Table 5-4 presents these results.

Two of the six variables—the variance of CR attitudes and the modal proportion of SW attitudes—are significantly related to House winning margins. As predicted, a Representative's expected vote increases as the proportion in the modal category on the SW scale increases, and decreases as the variance of CR attitudes increases. Thus, a Representative whose constituency is completely like-minded on these two dimensions expects to receive

$$y = .71 + .30(1) - .14(0) = 1.01 \text{ or}$$

101 percent of the vote, a theoretically pleasing, if numerically impossible, conclusion.

Interestingly, with either measure, homogeneity along only one dimension bears a significant relationship to electoral margin, but the dimensions differ for the two measures. Using the interval statistic, var, homogeneity on the CR dimension appears to be most closely associated with safety. But using the ordinal statistic, $\overline{m}$, homogeneity on the SW dimension appears to be related most closely to safety. Here is an example of how an a priori choice of measures could amount to an a priori choice of conclusions.

Mindful of the earlier Senate results, we have used a more elaborate regression model to reestimate the relationship between House election margins and district

Table 5-4
House Winners' Proportions as a Function of District Attitudinal Homogeneity (I)

Variable	B	σ_B	R^2	a	s.e.e.
CR var	−.14	.06	.16	.71	.17
SW $\overline{m}$	.30	.15			

attitudinal homogeneity. This model is analogous to (5.1) in allowing the regression intercepts and diversity slopes to vary between South and non-South. These more illuminating results appear in Table 5-5.

Table 5-5 contains several points worth noting. First, as predicted, the signs of the significant homogeneity variables are positive. The overall relationship between homogeneity and electoral margin is somewhat stronger in the House than in the Senate. Moreover, this stronger relationship is due solely to district homogeneity variables: the South and incumbency dummies are not significant in the House analysis. Rather, for Northern Representatives one has simply

$$\text{Winners' Proportion} = .47 + .22(\,\text{CR}\overline{m}\,)$$

and for Southerners,

$$\text{Winners' Proportion} = .47 + .40(\,\text{CR}\overline{m}\,) + .41(\text{SW}\overline{m}\,).$$

Substantively, we find that the CR dimension is important in both South and non-South, while the SW dimension also figures in the South prediction equation. The FA dimension fails to be significant in either South or non-South. These conclusions dovetail nicely with those of Miller and Stokes. Just as CR and SW issues find Representatives most in agreement with their constituents, so these dimensions are those on which constituency heterogeneity bodes ill for the Representatives.

Tables 5-2 and 5-5 show that electoral safety is associated with district homogeneity, although the relevant dimensions of the latter may differ between regions. Only one question remains: Are safety and homogeneity related closely enough that our theory may be interpreted as a theory of the roll-call voting of representatives from safe and marginal districts? We offer a tentative yes. Because the strengths of the relationships reported leave something to be desired, we will elaborate on this positive conclusion.

The data analysis summarized in Tables 5-2 and 5-5 represents, we believe, the first systematic attempt to explain district safety or marginality. (Customarily, one explains safety by noting a whole lot of Democrats or Republicans on

Table 5-5
House Winners' Proportions as a Function of District Attitudinal Homogeneity (II)

Variable	B	σ_B	R^2	a	s.e.e.
Southern SW $\overline{m}$	.41	.15			
Southern CR $\overline{m}$	.40	.18	.60	.47	.12
Non-Southern CR $\overline{m}$	.22	.12			

the registration rolls.) Because this study is exploratory we have used only existing data and simple, obvious measures. We have relied on demographic data in one case and very small district samples in the other. Thus, measurement and sampling error may affect our results significantly. Moreover, even with better data, district homogeneity may be a hard concept to pin down. What are the most important dimensions of political cleavage? These dimensions conceivably could be idiosyncratic to individual legislative districts. Certainly, one of the main weapons of the political challenger is to find a cleavage—any cleavage—to exploit.

Additionally, the concept of safety used in our theory depends on probabilities of reelection, not proportion of the vote. Empirically, one has little choice but to use the latter, although percentage of the vote may relate but tenuously to probability of victory.

Thus, the relationships reported in Tables 5-2 and 5-5 must be evaluated in light of weaknesses in the data and measures. In this light we believe that sufficient evidence has been presented in this section to justify considering our theory as an analysis of voting in safe and marginal districts as well as (better, because it is) an analysis of voting in homogeneous and heterogeneous districts. Of course, much more research should be done on the correspondence of safe-marginal to various dimensions of homogeneity-heterogeneity. But, until more work has been completed, we will assume the empirical correspondence of the two dimensions and see what comes of it.

The Myth of the Moderate
Marginal Representative

In Chapter 1 we took note of the hypothesis that electoral competition exerts a moderating influence on roll-call voting behavior. According to several researchers, representatives from competitive districts can and to some extent do enhance their chances of reelection by taking moderate, middle-of-the-road positions, an argument consistent with existing models of party competition which find candidate convergence a pervasive feature of electoral politics. On the other hand, Samuel Huntington has argued that the nature of party competition in marginal districts leads representatives from those districts to eschew the middle ground and stake out a position far from the center of the constituency preference distribution. Seldom does such a clear contradiction occur in the professional literature.

Until now we have been unable to choose between the two competing hypotheses. For, the data gathered to test these hypotheses are singularly irrelevant to the task. The hypotheses refer to the position a legislator takes within the electoral arena—his district. But characterizations of policy positions invariably are based on comparisons made within the legislative arena. And whether a representative looks conservative relative to his fellow legislators in principle tells us nothing about whether he looks conservative relative to his constituents. Thus, despite several research attempts an interesting question remains unanswered.

On the basis of the simple model described in Chapters 2-4 we are inclined to agree with Huntington. The logic is not completely obvious so we will spell it out. First, if two constituency groups are approximately equal in the probability that they care about an issue, then a maximizer votes exclusively with the stronger group, while a maintainer does so with probability greater than one-half. Second, we suspect that, empirically, representatives from very competitive districts would be precisely those who would be less certain of reelection than they would like to be, i.e., $p < p^*$. Thus, representatives from very competitive districts will likely be maximizers.[e] Third, if the constituency group structure stays constant from issue to issue, as it would if the relevant constituency groups were the constituency parties, then we would find maximizers voting always with the stronger constituency party (presumably theirs, since they were elected). Thus, we would expect marginal representatives to show a close allegiance to their constituency party, and to the extent that marginal districts are conflictual in their group structure one would expect this allegiance to draw these representatives away from the middle ground in the district.

One might bear in mind, of course, that the driving factor in our argument is not electoral competition, but district heterogeneity. Huntington, too, appears to regard heterogeneity as fundamental in that it determines the nature of party competition. On the other hand, the arguments which suggest that competition produces moderation tend to regard electoral competition as more of an independent variable in its own right.

Well, political scientists as well as nature abhor vacuums, so we will attempt to answer the question raised in this section. In highly competitive districts does one find convergence, divergence, neither or both? In the remainder of this section we shall present and discuss a new set of data which is most provocative. This data set appears to vindicate Huntington and support our argument. Additionally, it raises very interesting questions about existing models of electoral competition and their preoccupation with candidate convergence. As with the marginality hypothesis, the reality of electoral competition appears to be strikingly different from the conclusions advanced in existing studies.

In their text William Keefe and Morris Ogul cite a study in which Judith Strain presents a surprising finding.[13] Her data concern the voting behavior of Representatives from marginal-switch (M-S) districts, i.e., marginal districts

---

[e]Additionally, one would expect "newer" representatives (i.e., those with few electoral victories) to be maximizers. To the extent that turnover is most frequent in marginal districts, those districts will be represented by newer legislators. Thus, for a second reason one may suggest that representatives from competitive districts tend to be maximizers.

which underwent changes in party control between two Congresses. The average *difference* in Conservative Coalition support between the incumbents of the 86th Congress, 2nd Session, and the 87th Congress, 1st Session was 73 percent! "In almost every case the Democrat replacing a Republican or the Republican replacing a Democrat gave the constituency an entirely different 'brand' of representation on major policy questions."[14] If these data are reliable, they refute decisively the hypothesis that keen electoral competition results in identical parties. The seventeen districts Strain studied clearly were not electing men who voted in moderate, middle-of-the-road fashion.

Strain's method strikes us as the best available for measuring the differences in voting strategy between two candidates *within* a given constituency. Granted, individuality is uncontrolled, the particular roll calls differ from Congress to Congress, and the overall political context changes. Still, short of going into each constituency and interviewing, cross-Congress comparisons of voting behavior in switch districts appear to be the best way of estimating within-constituency policy differences in those districts.

Happily, some recent elections have produced numerous marginal-switch districts. We have gathered voting data on 42 such districts for the 88th-89th Congresses, and 32 for the 89th-90th Congresses.[15] If Huntington's critics are correct, the 40 M-S Democrats who came into office with Lyndon Johnson did not create a large break with the Republicans they replaced. And Huntington's critics again would be correct if the 31 M-S Republicans elected in 1966 voted similarly to the Democrats they replaced. On the other hand, if Huntington is correct, Strain's finding should be replicated: the different Representatives responded exclusively to the stronger constituency party.[f] Which is the case? Table 5-6 should help us decide.

Truly, the sheer magnitude of the voting shifts is staggering. On the average, the switch in parties from the 88th to the 89th Congresses was accompanied by a change of over 60 percent in support for the Conservative Coalition, and over 50 percent in support for a Larger Federal Role. Of course, many will point out that the 88th Congress was partly a Kennedy Congress, while the 89th was a Johnson Congress. Additionally, an assassination and an aberrant election intervened between the two Congresses. But the findings for the 89th-90th Congresses are basically the same.

Furthermore, consider the 16 *double* M-S districts which were taken from the Republicans by the Democrats, and wrested back again by the Republicans. The data for these districts appear in Table 5-7.

Now, we pose the question; Do the data in Tables 5-6 and 5-7 support the contention that Representatives from marginal districts vote in moderate, middle-of-the-road fashion? Hardly. Instead we see a picture of "flip-flopping"

---

[f]We assume, of course, that the party victorious in the preceding election constitutes the stronger constituency party.

Table 5-6

Mean Changes in Voting Support for the Conservative Coalition and a Larger Federal Role in M-S Districts,[†] 88th, 89th, and 90th Congresses[‡]

Congresses	Mean Change in CC Support	Mean Change in LFR Support	
88th-89th	60.5% (61.4)*	51.4% (51.2)	$n = 42$ (37)*
89th-90th	54.7% (57.6)	40.1% (42.8)	$n = 32$ (29)
All	58.0% (59.7)	46.5% (47.4)	$n = 74$ (66)

*Figures in parentheses are based only on those districts in which the replacement defeated the incumbent. In a few districts, the incumbents retired, or suffered primary defeats.

[†]A relevant question concerns the possible effects of redistricting on the voting shifts reported in row 2 of Table 5-6. During the 89th Congress there was extensive redistricting throughout the country in the wake of Wesberry vs. Sanders. Thus, some of the districts comprising the data base for row 2 of the table underwent some boundary change between the 89th and 90th Congresses. We cannot say to what extent the voting shifts resulted from redistricting. Note, however, that the even greater voting changes for the 88th to 89th Congresses are not so subject to the redistricting question. Moreover, John Ferejohn has compiled data extending from the 84th to the 88th Congresses which show similar large shifts, albeit with fewer cases.

[‡]As an incidental point, these whole-Congress comparisons do not mask any intersession voting differences. For example, the average Conservative Coalition score of the 31 M-S Democrats differed only 2.3 percent between 1965 and 1966.

Source: *Congressional Quarterly Almanac*, 1964, 1966, 1967.

representation. The representatives from these districts represent their part of the constituency and the devil take the other. Extremes replace extremes.

Of course, various explanations for the data can be advanced. In the context of the present discussion, though, the data are quite consistent with Huntington's theory and our arguments. To be sure, we have not tested Huntington's theory completely, because we present no data on policy differences within safe districts. By definition, safe-switch districts are rare, so a measurement problem exists. But, consider the kind of world which would produce policy differences between candidates in safe districts greater than the reported differences between candidates in marginal districts. Such a world would find (1) flaming liberal Republicans running against the safe Southern Democrats, (2) rock-ribbed conservative Republicans running in the metropolitan Northern Democratic strongholds, (3) "radiclib" Democrats opposing safe Republicans in the heartland. Should one expect these phenomena to come to pass in sufficient numbers to beat the spreads reported in Table 5-6? To say the least, the prospect is doubtful.

Actually, one can use some rather weak data to measure directly the policy differences between candidates in safe districts. Let us define a "safe-switch" district as one which shifts parties between two Congresses, but by a margin of more than 55 percent. There were eight such districts between the 88th and

Table 5-7

Percentage Support for the Conservative Coalition and a Larger Federal Role in Double M-S Districts, 88th, 89th, and 90th Congresses†

District*	CC Support			LFR Support		
	88	89	90	88	89	90
Colorado 2 (Boulder)	93	14	72	56	87	59
Illinois 19 (Rock Island)	81	14	57	33	83	59
Iowa 1 (Iowa City)	44	10	62	50	78	45
Iowa 4 (Southcentral)	67	18	90	39	73	23
Michigan 2 (Ann Arbor)	56	5	52	33	96	73
Michigan 11 (Upper Peninsula)	81	1	51	39	100	68
Nebraska 1 (Lincoln)	93	34	88	0	78	32
New Jersey 2 (Atlantic City)	67	1	70	67	100	59
North Dakota 2 (Western)	81	25	81	11	91	32
Ohio 1 (Cincinnati)	74	3	51	50	96	64
Ohio 3 (Dayton)	81	8	27	50	91	77
Ohio 10 (Southeastern)	85	34	92	22	73	23
Pennsylvania 19 (York)	89	14	94	22	91	23
Wisconsin 1 (Racine)	96	14	91	22	91	32
Wisconsin 6 (Sheboygan)	74	26	69	28	87	55
Wyoming AL	93	5	72	28	65	32

*In parentheses we attempt to give some indication of the location of these districts within their respective states.

†Some of these districts are worthy of tracing even further back. Consider the fascinating Pennsylvania 19th for example.

Year	Winner	Party	Margin	CC Score
'52	Stauffer	R	52.3%	n.a.
'54	Quigley	D	51.0%	n.a.
'56	Stauffer	R	53.8%	n.a.
'58	Quigley	D	51.5%	3%

Table 5-7 (cont.)

Year	Winner	Party	Margin	CC Score
'60	Goodling	R	53.2%	87%
'62	Goodling	R	56.8%	89%
'64	Craley	D	50.8%	14%
'66	Goodling	R	51.7%	94%
'68	Goodling	R	57.7%	87%
'70	Goodling	R	54.0%	85%

This district underwent no boundary change until 1972, yet it remained marginal through two Presidential landslides (1956, 1964) and three Congressional landslides (1958, 1964, 1966). As of 1970 the Republicans had about a 12 percent registration edge. If we can assume that Quigley voted in the 84th Congress as he did in the 86th and that Stauffer compiled a record similar to Goodling's, then the people of the Pennsylvania 19th were treated to six across the spectrum shifts in policy representation between 1952 and 1968.

89th Congresses, and 20 between the 89th and 90th Congresses. Classing such districts as "safe" presents conceptual difficulties, mainly because of the party switch, but also because 18 of the 28 districts were won by less than 60 percent of the vote. But, ignoring such difficulties, consider Table 5-8 and contrast it to Table 5-6.

In every case the average voting shift in the "safe-switch" districts falls short of the average shifts in the M-S districts. According to Huntington, as the quantitative difference between the constituency parties increases, the qualitative difference decreases. Judging by Tables 5-6, 5-8 and our argument of the preceding paragraph, Huntington appears to be correct for the 88th-90th Congresses.

What, then, of findings to the effect that representatives from marginal districts are more moderate than their compatriots from safe districts? Upon consideration it is clear that such findings in no way conflict with Huntington's theory, our model, or the data in Tables 5-6 and 5-7. For, *"moderate relative to one's fellow legislators"* does not logically imply *"moderate relative to one's constituency."* A marginal representative can be utterly loyal to one segment of

Table 5-8
Mean Changes in Voting Support for the Conservative Coalition and a Larger Federal Role in Safe-Switch Districts, 88th, 89th, and 90th Congresses

Congresses	Mean Change in CC Support	Mean Change in LFR Support	
88th-89th	42.1%	48.5%	*n* = 8
89th-90th	42.4%	32.8%	*n* = 20
All	42.3%	37.3%	*n* = 28

Source: *Congressional Quarterly Almanac*, 1964, 1966, 1967.

his district and yet be more or less extreme (or equally so) than his fellow legislative partisans, depending, of course, on the position of his fellow partisans vis-à-vis the favored segment of his district. For example, consider the preference distributions illustrated in Figure 5-1, which might symbolize the Massachusetts or Pennsylvania situations.[g]

Note that according to our model a leftist candidate in the marginal district favors legislative proposal *B*. This is near the preferred position of the stronger constituency group, and not a moderate, middle-of-the-road proposal such as *C*. Yet observers would rate this representative as moderate *in comparison to a safe colleague* who favors proposal *A*.

On the other hand, examine Figure 5-2. In this case a marginal representative who behaves in accord with our model favors proposal *A*. But now one would judge him as extreme both relative to his constituency, and *relative to a safe colleague* who favors proposal *B*.

To sum up, we reject the notion that marginal representatives adopt moderate, compromise positions aimed at pleasing all sectors of the constituency. Instead, the data support the argument based on the model developed in

Figure 5-1. Illustration of the Constituency Extremism and Legislative Moderation of a Marginal Representative.

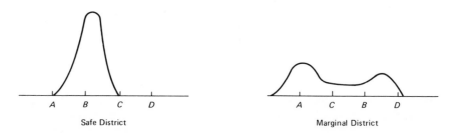

Figure 5-2. Illustration of the Constituency Extremism and Legislative Extremism of a Marginal Representative.

[g]These preference distributions are purely for illustrative purposes. We introduce them without assuming any of the myriad axioms and theorems found in the spatial modeling literature.

Chapters 2-4: marginal representatives align with the stronger group. Huntington's theory also finds support in the data inasmuch as it makes much the same prediction as our theory. But, bear in mind that neither Huntington's theory nor ours predicts that marginal representatives take any more or less extreme policy positions than safe representatives. Such hypotheses refer to *cross-district comparisons* rather than *within-district comparisons*. The two theories discussed deal only with the latter. As Figures 5-1 and 5-2 make clear, cross-district relationships depend on factors other than the strategies pursued within the separate constituencies.

Before closing this discussion we offer a conjecture. In Chapter 1 we remarked that studies of state legislatures find party deviation related to marginality. This finding in turn suggests that marginal representatives are moderate with respect to their fellow legislative partisans. On the other hand, scholars have not found deviation and marginality related among Congressmen. And our data give no indication that marginal Congressmen are any more moderate in their policy positions than their colleagues.[h] We suggest that Figure 5-1 reflects the situation in most states. Each party finds a home in basically one type of district, e.g., urban vs. rural. The safe seats in each party are quite similar. In contrast, the competitive seats occur in areas not typical of either party. Furthermore, the parties in the competitive districts are not typical of their corresponding entities in the safe districts. For example, a suburban Republican party may not want to build rural roads, or ban liquor sales at the metropolitan stadium. Similarly, the suburban Democratic party may not be ecstatic about open housing legislation pushed by the majority of their party colleagues from big city safe districts. Figure 5-1 would appear to represent the situation outlines. We would expect to find the marginal representatives both deviating from party, and taking more moderate positions than their fellow legislative party members.

On the other hand, in the Congress neither party finds its support exclusively in one type of district, especially the Democratic Party.[16] Thus, no majority in the party from nearly identical districts can set up their constituency interests as the party position. Rather, the party position itself must be a compromise. In this situation there is much less reason to expect deviation on the part of the marginal representatives. Nor should we expect them to appear more moderate than their fellow party members. Sometimes they might appear more extreme, sometimes less extreme, and sometimes equally extreme. All of the preceding is,

---

[h]For example, in the 89th Congress the 40 M-S northern Democrats had average Conservative Coalition and Larger Federal Role Support Scores of 11 percent and 87 percent, respectively. The 163 non-M-S northern Democrats had average scores of 12 percent and 89 percent. In the 90th Congress the 31 M-S Republicans had average Conservative Coalition and Larger Federal Support Scores of 72 percent and 44 percent, respectively, while the 155 non-M-S Republicans had average scores of 69 percent and 44 percent. In these two Congresses, at least, the M-S and non-M-S Representatives were virtually indistinguishable in their voting behavior. (See Table 5-9.)

of course, highly tentative and nonrigorous. But after a long immersion in theory, data, and the literature, the above is our explanation of the fact that marginality and party deviation are sometimes related, and sometimes not.

Digressions aside, we restate the major point of this section: *marginal representatives may be less extreme partisans than their safe colleagues, but this does not imply that they adopt moderate, middle-of-the-road positions within their constituencies. Rather, they represent almost exclusively one segment of the constituency.*

Table 5-9

Comparative Support for the Conservative Coalition and a Larger Federal Role, M-S v. Non-M-S Representatives, 89th and 90th Congresses

89th Congress (Northern Democrats)	M-S	Non-M-S
C.C. Support	11%	11%
LFR Support	87%	89%
	(*n*=40)	(*n*=163)
90th Congress (Republicans)		
C.C. Support	72%	69%
LFR Support	44%	44%
	(*n*=31)	(*n*=155)

Conclusion: M-S Representatives in the 89th and 90th Congresses were neither more nor less extreme in their policy positions than other Representatives.

The Miller Data

In Chapter 1 we discussed the sharp contradiction between Miller's Congressional study and the marginality hypothesis. Miller found—to the surprise of many—that Congressmen from one-party districts represented their majority party constituents on civil rights and social welfare questions far better than did Congressmen from marginal districts. Additionally, safe Congressmen had more accurate perceptions of constituents' preferences than did marginal Congressmen, safe Congressmen voted their perceptions more so than marginal Congressmen, and safe Congressmen were less likely to vote their own attitudes than were marginal Congressmen. We hope that our arguments in Chapter 1 have convinced the reader that the marginality hypothesis is no more than a hypothesis—one whose apparent confirmation depended on an unjustified inference. But we are still left with Miller's findings which, at first glance, seem as counterintuitive as the marginality hypothesis seemed intuitively plausible. We have argued that our analysis provides a theory of the voting behavior of safe and marginal representatives. Can this theory shed some light on Miller's findings? This question charts our course in this section.

To begin, consider the argument that the notions of safe and competitive only reflect an underlying homogeneity or heterogeneity of constituents' preferences. This simple correspondence makes several of Miller's findings plausible, indeed, expected. For example, Congressmen from marginal districts less accurately perceive majority preferences than do their safe colleagues (.11 vs. .38 in SW; .23 vs. .78 in CR). Is not such a finding plausible if, in fact, safe districts are homogeneous—characterized by an overwhelmingly dominant set of ideas, whereas marginal districts are heterogeneous—characterized by conflicting interests?[1][7]

Consider that the attitudes of safe representatives correspond more closely to the attitudes of majority constituents than do the attitudes of marginal representatives (.39 vs. .27 in SW; .54 vs. −.16 in CR). Indeed, the attitudes of safe representatives also correspond more closely to the attitudes of *minority* constituents than do the attitudes of marginal representatives (.26 vs. −.38 in SW; .31 vs. −.14 in CR). In fact, the attitudes of safe representatives correspond as closely to the attitudes of *minority* constituents as the attitudes of marginal representatives correspond to the attitudes of *majority* constituents in SW (.26 vs. .27) and *more closely* in CR (.31 vs. −.16)! These rather cryptic relationships are somewhat less puzzling if the hypothesized relationship holds between district homogeneity and safety, and heterogeneity and marginality.

And what of Miller's important finding that the supposed free agent, the "trustee" from the safe district turns out in fact to be a rather faithful representative? From a theoretical standpoint one should not be surprised. In Chapter 3 we showed that maximizers from homogeneous districts always vote with their constituents, while maintainers from such districts vote with their constituents with probability at least Q, where $.5 \leqslant Q \leqslant 1.0$. Of course, crude operational definitions of safety would also include heterogeneous districts in which one group clearly dominates. But given $c_1 = c_2$ maximizers from heterogeneous districts always vote with the dominant group. Similarly, we know that maintainers from such districts vote with the dominant group with probability at least Q, where $.5 < Q \leqslant 1.0$. Thus, safe districts notwithstanding, both maximizers and maintainers will be found voting with their dominant constituency groups with minimum probability $.5 + \epsilon$, and usually considerably higher. In light of these propositions, correlations of .60 (SW) and .64 (CR) between safe representatives' votes and majority constituents' preferences are not so unexpected. Certainly, the usual leap from electoral safety to voting freedom gives too little credit to the electorate. Are we to assume that voters are boobs who continue to support representatives who fail to represent them? Political champions are made, not born. A representative can build up safety, but conversely, if he eschews use of optimal voting strategies, he may find himself fighting for his electoral life—or losing it.

Having interpreted Miller's findings for safe representatives in terms of our model, consider now the perplexing findings for marginal representatives. There is simply no relation (.08 in SW, −.08 in CR) between marginal representatives' votes and their majority constituents' preferences. At the outset we admit that these findings trouble us much more than the findings for safe representatives.

The only easy way to explain the total lack of relationship would be to assert that Miller's marginal representatives see their constituencies as so evenly divided that they have no gainful voting strategies. In such an event, they might give up hope of reelection, and pursue the true and beautiful, or make hay while the sun shines. But, besides being an intellectual copout of rather large order, such an explanation is inconsistent with the voting behavior of marginal representatives discussed in the preceding section of this chapter. What, then? At least two other possibilities must be considered.

First, one might discount the data. An average of 17 constituents per Congressional district were interviewed. And while Miller and Stokes defend the accuracy of estimates based on these small samples in "Constituency Influence in Congress," one does seem justified in questioning the accuracy of the population estimates when the small samples are subdivided into majority and minority.[18] In closely divided districts an average of nine respondents would be the basis of "majority constituents' attitudes." In safe districts, where "majority constituents" tend to coincide with all constituents interviewed, the problem is somewhat less severe. So, at least some doubts about the marginal district data are warranted.

Second, the amorphous group, "majority party constituents," may not be the relevant constituency group in marginal districts. The theory may be correct, and Miller's data may be correct, and yet the two might not bear on each other. Of course, one must be wary of searching for new "truly relevant constituency groups" whenever troublesome data appear. Such fancy footwork results in theories which are not falsifiable. Nevertheless, we think there exists a plausible argument that the "majority constituents" interviewed by the Survey Research Center are not the relevant constituency group for the marginal Representative. We will proceed to outline this argument.[19]

Some have suggested that the importance of the political party varies directly with electoral competition. In a one-party area, the correct party label, a modicum of propriety, adequate constituency service, and reasonable voting are sufficient to clinch renomination and election. In such a homogeneous area, no market exists for a challenger. He can only appeal to the same constituency as the incumbent. Thus, the incumbent finds himself in an advantaged position. Because the disaffected have nowhere to go, the incumbent need not worry too much about a few disaffected individuals, party activists or otherwise. He need only maintain the support of the average voter.

Conversely, in areas of keen electoral competition, party activists may take on importance far beyond their numbers. Since he usually estimates a non-negligible probability of defeat, the representative cannot easily write-off any sources of support, least of all campaign workers. Because of their activities, party activists have "weighted" votes: The support of an activist can generally be translated into several ordinary votes. In homogeneous districts where the representative wins by 70-30, the loss of a few votes, even weighted ones, is not crucial. In heterogeneous districts where the representative wins by 52-48, loss of party activist support may assure defeat.

These arguments suggest, to use Sorauf's terms, that the party in the electorate counts more in one-party areas, while the party activists count more in competitive areas.[20] The crucial link in the argument is the oft-made observation that party activists are not representative of party identifiers generally.[21] As in other types of groups, the activist members tend to be more aware of group activities, more committed to group goals, more appreciative of group membership, etc. Translated into political terms, the activists tend to be more aware of partisan issues and more committed to party positions. Most importantly, they tend to be more extreme in their positions than the less committed party identifiers, especially Republican activists.[22] The 1964 Republican national convention and campaign illustrates most dramatically the gulf between activists and identifiers.[23] And the data may yet show that 1972 illustrates a newly emerged similar phenomenon for Democrats.

Returning now to the Survey Research Center data one may hypothesize that majority party preferences as seen by the marginal Congressman differ from majority party preferences as ascertained by the Survey Research Center. For a start, one might expect that marginal Republican Congressmen and the activists would be out of step with Republican identifiers on social welfare issues, while marginal Democratic Congressmen and activists would be out of step with Democratic identifiers on CR issues. No doubt when a marginal Democrat thinks of AFL-CIO support for his campaign, he thinks in terms of pleasing the union hierarchy, not the assembly-line worker interviewed by the Survey Research Center. But, while labor lobbyists push CR bills on Capitol Hill, the men they "represent" may be stoning CR marchers in Illinois.

None of the above is meant as criticism of Miller's work. His finding still stands: marginal Congressmen do not seem to represent those who are ostensibly their "constituents." Still, one cannot infer consequently that marginal Congressmen represent no one. In particular, we would caution against Miller's suggestion that they vote their own preferences. Obviously, Congressmen are themselves party activists. Thus, their preferences may coincide with the preferences of the constituents (activists) they seek to represent, making separate study of the two possible influences difficult. Perhaps marginal Congressmen so poorly perceive constituency preferences because they think in terms of the majority party activists. Perhaps, too, the reason why the personal attitudes of marginal Congressmen correspond so poorly to the attitudes of constituents lies in the fact that the Congressman is an activist, and not an ordinary constituent.

The argument we have presented is by no means conclusive. It may be only a convenient way to accommodate the theory to some contrary data. But the literature of political parties lends some plausibility to the argument, and the theory, after all, does not say that the representative must respond to majority party identifiers. The theory predicts only that a representative responds to the strongest constituency group, *as he perceives it*. Ascertaining the relevant groups is an empirical question, for which we have offered an empirical answer. At this time nothing suggests that both Miller's data and the theoretical propositions cannot be simultaneously valid.

Abstention: Hypotheses and Data

In Chapter 4 we derived a number of conclusions concerning representatives' use of the abstention strategy. Specifically, if the c_j estimates are nonzero,

1. Maximizers from homogeneous constituencies never abstain.
2. Maintainers from homogeneous constituencies may be able to profit both electorally and in terms of secondary goals by abstaining with some positive probability.
3. Maximizers from heterogeneous constituencies may encounter situations in which abstention is their loss-minimization strategy.
4. Maintainers from heterogeneous constituencies may abstain with some positive probability, depending on the secondary goals associated with abstention and casting a vote.

The import of these four propositions is quite interesting. If we could classify representatives according to consensual and conflictual constituency type and maximizing and maintaining motivation, then isolate a set of votes for which $c_j > 0$, the theory tells us that abstention rates among the homogeneous maximizers will be less than or equal to abstention rates among the other three classes. Of course, classifying representatives, and isolating a relevant set of votes is no mean trick. Nevertheless, we have made the attempt. In this section we report the results of an attempt to test predictions 1 - 4. Our test is extremely crude. In the absence of interview data we utilize heroic auxiliary assumptions about the relationships of homogeneous-heterogeneous and maximizer-maintainer to more easily measured variables, and also about the roll calls on which $c_j > 0$.

Auxiliary Assumption 1: First and second term Congressmen are maximizers; more senior Congressmen are maintainers.

It seems plausible that a Congressman who has only survived one or two elections will still find $p < p^*$ (provided p^* is set fairly high to reflect a high subjective value for the Congressional seat). Even if he has won by large margins, probably he has not yet solidified his position, not yet achieved the status of a fixture, or institution. Conversely, electorally more experienced Congressmen are more likely to have established a stable position vis-à-vis the district. Of course, AA-1 is a gross oversimplification, and choice of the third election rather than the second or fourth is somewhat arbitrary.

Auxiliary Assumption 2: Congressmen who win by 55 percent or less represent heterogeneous districts; those who win by 65 percent or more represent homogeneous districts.

Obviously, AA-2 is based on our earlier arguments. Those Congressmen winning by margins of 56-64 percent are not included in an attempt to get relatively pure instances of heterogeneous and homogeneous districts.

Auxiliary assumptions 1 and 2 enable us to divide the world into four very rough categories. Table 5-10 illustrates the classification. Of the four cells (2, 1) inspires the least confidence. We suspect that many Congressmen from marginal

Table 5-10
Classification of Congressmen by Homogeneity of District and Electoral Motivation

	Heterogeneous ($\leqslant 55\%$)	Homogeneous ($\leqslant 65\%$)
Maximizer ($\leqslant 2$)	Heterogeneous Maximizer	Homogeneous Maximizer
Maintainer (> 2)	Heterogeneous Maintainer ?	Homogeneous Maintainer

districts remain maximizers despite several victories. Thus, the heterogeneous maintainer category may very well contain mostly heterogeneous maximizers. In view of this ambiguity we have chosen to ignore prediction 4. In the tables which follow, predictions 1 - 3 are examined: only cells (1, 1) and 2, 2) are compared to (1, 2).

Auxiliary Assumption 3: $c_j > 0$ for all votes.

By making the third auxiliary assumption we assert that a Congressman believes that *every* vote has some nonzero probability of becoming a campaign issue. The assumption may not be all that outlandish when one considers that opponents are free to misconstrue the meaning and significance of the incumbent's votes.[24] With the third auxiliary assumption in effect, we can make comparisons of Congressmen's total abstention rates over all the votes in a Congress.

As a measure of abstention, we have employed 100 percent minus the *Congressional Quarterly* On the Record Score. The *Congressional Quarterly* On the Record Score includes live pairs and announced positions (e.g., statements in the *Congressional Record*) as well as actual roll-call cast. For several reasons we have chosen this measure over the *Congressional Quarterly* Voting Participation score, which counts only actual votes cast. Almost all Congressmen are absent on occasion from Congress. In addition to sickness and other personal reasons, Congressmen may travel on Congressional business (or the appearance thereof) and most try to spend a considerable amount of time in their districts. Thus, few Congressmen can avoid missing one or more roll calls during a given Congress. But one should not equate *absences* with *abstentions.* If the Congressman goes to the trouble to arrange a live pair or otherwise make his position public, he is not abstaining in the sense of the abstention strategy in the theory. The latter involves taking no position in support of either side on the issue. Moreover, from the standpoint of the theory it matters little whether the Representative actually votes or merely announces his position. Even the latter puts a weapon into the hands of his opponents:

I worried about debating on the floor and the fact that I had never had any experience in such matters. After a year or so in Congress I went to my committee chairman who was a very good speaker and told him I was concerned. I wondered what he thought about the fact I hadn't made any speeches on the floor. He said, "let me tell you something, son. No congressman has ever been defeated by a speech he didn't make on the floor of the House." I have thought about it many times because the man who told me was defeated after many years by speeches he did make on the floor. Words were thrown back to him that he had spoken twenty years before.[25]

For these reasons, then, we believe that the *Congressional Quarterly* On the Record Score gives a better estimate of the use of the abstention strategy than does a score based on roll-call votes alone.

The data in Table 5-12 are based on 177 roll calls from the first session of the 91st Congress.[i] Table 5-11 summarizes the party breakdown of the categories analyzed. With the exception of the heterogeneous maximizers the two parties appear in the table in rough proportion to their strength in the Congress (56 percent Democratic, 44 percent Republican).

The distributions of abstention rates are so highly skewed that average

Table 5-11
Party Breakdown of Categories Analyzed (91:1)*

Type of Representative	Democrats	Republicans
Homogeneous Maximizers ($n = 38$)	58%	42%
Homogeneous Maintainers ($n = 143$)	60%	40%
Heterogeneous Maximizers ($n = 35$)	34%	66%

*The data summarized in Tables 5-11 to 5-16 are drawn from the annual *Congressional Quarterly Almanacs.*

Table 5-12
Abstention Among Categories of Representative, 91:1 (177 roll calls)

Type of Representative	0	0-5	10+
Homogeneous Maximizer	34%	82%	11%
Homogeneous Maintainer	31%	62%	26%
Heterogeneous Maximizer	27%	78%	5%

[i]All the data we present come from the first sessions of the relevant Congresses. During the second session (election year) Congressmen are typically less conscientious about their legislative work, devoting much time to their campaigns. Thus we feel that the first session voting results yield a purer estimate of voting patterns.

abstention scores have little meaning; therefore, we list several facts about the distributions in Table 5-12.

Evidently, prediction 1 is not confirmed. Nowhere near 100 percent of the homogeneous maximizers had abstention rates of zero. Of course, the auxiliary assumptions certainly introduce some error into the test, so the failure to confirm a prediction of an exact value is not particularly disturbing. If one grants only a 5 percent allowance for the grossness of the test, we find that the overwhelming bulk (82 percent) of the homogeneous maximizers meet this less stringent criterion.

Predictions 2 and 3 fare rather well. All across the board homogeneous maintainers compile higher abstention rates than homogeneous maximizers. The heterogeneous maximizers abstain at rates very similar to the homogeneous maximizers. Admittedly, the differences in abstention rates are not large, but the theory does not say they should be.[j] The theory specifies only that abstention by those listed in row 1 of the table shall not *exceed* abstention by those listed in rows 2 and 3. Even equality is admissable under the theory. Interestingly, the only category in which abstention is more than a loss minimization strategy (homogeneous maintainers) clearly compiles the highest abstention rate.

In view of the grossness of the empirical test, one naturally expresses skepticism about the degree to which the data support the theoretical predictions. Suppose we placed Congressmen into seemingly irrelevant categories such as fat, normal, and skinny, and collected data on the respective abstention rates of the members of the three groups. Most of us would believe that abstention by the members of each group would be just as likely to be greater than as to be less than abstention by the members of the other groups (assuming the probability of exact equality equals zero). Purely on the basis of chance, however, there would be a .25 probability ($1/2 \times 1/2$) that abstention by the skinnies would be less than abstention by both the normals and fats. This finding would hardly impel us to launch an intensive investigation into the relationships between body build and voting behavior. If, however, one were to find that in Congress after Congress skinnies abstained less than fats and normals, one would grow increasingly confident that some real difference had been found. This is the strategy we have adopted.

In Tables 5-13 and 5-14 we present data for the first session of the 88th

Table 5-13
Party Breakdown of Categories Analyzed (88:1)

Type of Representative	Democrats	Republicans
Homogeneous Maximizers (n = 28)	79%	21%
Homogeneous Maintainers (n = 133)	79%	21%
Heterogeneous Maximizers (n = 45)	51%	49%

[j]Since the mean OR score for Representatives in the 91st Congress, first session, was 94 percent, the differences could not very well come out too large.

Table 5-14
Abstention Among Three Categories of Representative, 88:1 (119 Roll Calls)

Type of Representative	0	0-5	10+
Homogeneous Maximizers	25%	82%	4%
Homogeneous Maintainers	38%	68%	21%
Heterogeneous Maximizers	24%	73%	18%

Congress, the second Congress of John Kennedy's Presidency. Democrats are heavily overrepresented in the homogeneous categories, Republicans somewhat overrepresented among heterogeneous maximizers. Abstention scores are based on 119 roll calls.

Again, prediction 1 fares badly. In the first session of the 88th Congress homogeneous maximizers did not even have the greatest proportion of zero abstainers, let alone 100 percent. But, again, the overwhelming bulk (82 percent) meet the less stringent 0-5 percent standard. Predictions 2 and 3 appear to be supported a second time. Although homogeneous maintainers have the greatest proportion of zero abstainers, the latter are more than balanced out by the frequent (10+) abstainers. Heterogeneous maximizers abstain at a greater rate than homogeneous maximizers over all the abstention categories. The weight of the evidence grows a bit encouraging. Thus, we go back six more years to the first session of the 85th Congress in which the Democrats return to power in the House despite the Eisenhower landslide.

Table 5-16 is the sort of occurrence that sorely tries one's enthusiasm for

Table 5-15
Party Breakdown of Categories Analyzed (85:1)

Type of Representative	Democrats	Republicans
Homogeneous Maximizers (n = 32)	75%	25%
Homogeneous Maintainers (n = 132)	72%	28%
Heterogeneous Maximizers (n = 39)	67%	33%

Table 5-16
Abstention Among Three Categories of Representative, 85:1 (100 Roll Calls)

Type of Representative	0	0-5	10+
Homogeneous Maximizers	22%	44%	47%
Homogeneous Maintainers	17%	47%	33%
Heterogeneous Maximizers	18%	62%	15%

empirical testing. Although homogeneous maximizers have the greatest proportion of zero abstainers, the data cannot be interpreted to support the theoretical propositions. On the whole, abstention among our three categories of representative was higher in the 85th than in the 88th and 91st Congresses. More to the point, however, the homogeneous maximizers had shockingly high abstention rates (from the standpoint of the theory).

In sum, then, there is a tendency in two Congresses for Representatives to abstain in a manner consonant with the theoretical predictions. In a third Congress, however, we find contradictory evidence. The combination of mixed evidence and the grossness of the empirical test militates against any firm conclusion.

Summary and Conclusions

In this chapter we have reported several preliminary applications of the theory. Although a strict test of the theory will require direct estimates of the theoretical variables, the use of auxiliary assumptions enables one to bring existing data to bear on certain of the theoretical predictions. The four applications may be summarized as follows:

1. The theory implies that homogeneous constituencies tend to be safe electorally, while heterogeneous districts tend to be marginal, inasmuch as optimal voting strategies always exist in the former case but not in the latter. Tests using demographic and survey data produced generally positive results.
2. Marginal representatives do not adopt compromise, middle-of-the-road positions vis-à-vis their constituencies. Rather, consistent with the theoretical propositions, marginal representatives appear to align solidly with one side or the other of the constituency.
3. The puzzling findings of Warren Miller can be subsumed under the theoretical predictions, albeit some more easily than others. Miller's data contradict other theoretical formulations of which we are aware.
4. Some tendency exists for Congressmen to abstain along lines predicted by the theory. Some negative evidence was found, however.

In sum, these preliminary tests are not conclusive one way or the other. But, cumulatively, they seem sufficiently encouraging to suggest that we are at least heading in the right direction.

Notes

1. F.S.C. Northrup, *The Logic of the Sciences and the Humanities* (Cleveland: Meridian Books, 1947), Chapter VII.

2. James MacGregor Burns, *The Deadlock of Democracy* (Englewood Cliffs, N.J.: Prentice-Hall, 1963), p. 242.

3. For example, see V.O. Key, Jr.'s argument in *Politics, Parties, and Pressure Groups* (5th ed., New York: Crowell, 1964), p. 245. Key cites several studies in support of his argument.

4. Huntington, "A Revised Theory." Heinz Eulau, "The Ecological Basis of Party Systems: The Case of Ohio," *Midwest Journal of Political Science*, 1 (1957), 125-135.

5. Duane Lockard, *New England State Politics* (Princeton: Princeton University Press, 1959), p. 337.

6. Davidson, *The Role of the Congressman*, p. 128.

7. William Keefe, "The Functions and Powers of the State Legislature," in Alexander Heard (ed.), *State Legislatures in American Politics* (Englewood Cliffs, N.J.: Prentice-Hall, 1966), p. 43.

8. Kingdon, *Candidates for Office*, pp. 76-77.

9. Froman, *Congressmen and their Constituencies*, p. 121.

10. Huntington, "A Revised Theory," p. 676.

11. John Sullivan, "Political Correlates of Social, Economic and Religious Diversity in the American States," *Journal of Politics*, 35 (1973), 73.

12. Miller, "Majority Rule and the Representative System of Government," pp. 300-301.

13. William Keefe and Morris Ogul, *The American Legislative Process* (2nd ed., Englewood Cliffs, N.J.: Prentice-Hall, 1968), pp. 318-319.

14. Ibid.

15. Data for these classifications are drawn from the 1964, 1966 and 1967 *Congressional Quarterly Almanacs*. Following the usual convention, marginal districts are those carried by less than 55 percent of the vote.

16. Again, see David Mayhew, *Party Loyalty Among Congressmen*.

17. Jewell and Patterson make a similar argument in one of the few published discussions of the Miller findings. See Malcolm Jewell and Samuel Patterson, *The Legislative Process in the United States* (New York: Random House, 1966), pp. 439-444.

18. Miller and Stokes, footnote 3, pp. 33-34.

19. I am indebted to Professor Gordon Black for this argument. In a number of conversations he sketched the outlines for me. He develops it fully in a forthcoming book. See Gordon Black, *Parties, Elections, and Public Opinion* (New York: Worth, forthcoming, 1973), Chapter III. For a theoretical piece based on similar ideas, see Peter Aranson and Peter Ordeshook, "Spatial Strategies for Sequential Elections," in Niemi and Weisberg (eds.), *Probability Models in Political Science*.

20. Frank J. Sorauf makes the distinction between the party organization, the party in the electorate, and the party in government. See his *Party Politics in America* (Boston: Little, Brown, 1968), pp. 9-12.

21. The seminal article, of course, is Herbert McClosky, Paul Hoffman and Rosemary O'Hara, "Issue Conflict and Consensus Among Party Leaders and Followers," *American Political Science Review*, 54 (1960), 406-427.

22. Ibid. See also the 1964 data presented by John Kessel, *The Goldwater Coalition* (Indianapolis: Bobbs-Merrill, 1968), pp. 332-334.

23. Kessel, op. cit. See also Philip Converse, Aage Clausen, and Warren Miller, "Electoral Myth and Reality: The 1964 Election," *American Political Science Review*, 59 (1965), 321-336.

24. See former Congressman Frank Smith's discussion of the esoterica used against him by Congressman Jamie Whitten in their 1962 election fight. Frank Smith, *Congressman From Mississippi* (New York: Pantheon Books, 1964), pp. 288-289.

25. Clapp, *The Congressman*, p. 142.

Some Concluding Thoughts on Representative Democracy

Those who study the American voter or his representatives seldom can resist the temptation to utter some purportedly profound thoughts on the great normative questions of democratic theory—thoughts inspired by their research, of course. We will not break the tradition, if only because we disagree with some existing profundities. Assuming for the moment that the theory presented in preceding pages bears some relation to reality, what does it imply about the nature of representative democracy in the United States?

Two sets of theoretical implications stand out as most significant. The first set specifies to whom self-interested representatives respond, and to what degree. As such these propositions are the core of a theory of representation; they answer the question, "who, if anyone, gets represented?"

As we indicated, sometimes there is no particular reason to expect anyone to be represented. These are the situations in which representatives have no profitable strategies. They are damned if they do, and damned if they don't. Where representatives' predicaments are such that they have no nonlosing behavior open to them, representation may take on the character of a random phenomenon. A representative might seek to minimize his losses, or perhaps he votes on the basis of party, personal preferences or some other alternative grounds, and whatever representation occurs, results from a fortuitous consonance of some constituents' preferences and those of the alternative cue source.

Although we hereby travel far into the speculative realm, we would suggest that those who regard frequent electoral turnover as a prerequisite for faithful representation should rethink their position.[a] Such an argument is implicit, for example, in the judgments of those who discount constituency influence in the United States Congress because of the pronounced stability of the membership. It may be that the great bulk of Congressmen achieve reelection precisely *because* they vote optimally. On the contrary, the prospect of a likely defeat irrespective of his record probably will induce a hopeless attitude in the mind of the representative who frequently has only nonprofitable voting strategies. Electoral volatility could well produce the kind of haphazard, random represen-

[a]For example, in discussing San Francisco Bay Area City Councilman, Prewitt states that "The frequency with which officeholders are returned to office suggests that they are unlikely to be constantly preoccupied with voter preferences." In the absence of any accompanying conditions or assumptions we cannot help but regard such statements as nonsequiturs. See Kenneth Prewitt, "Political Ambitions, Volunteerism, and Electoral Accountability," *American Political Science Review*, 64 (1970), p. 10.

tation already mentioned. A representative must believe that by voting properly he can retain his seat. That is the hold the represented have on him. If he has no hope, that hold is gone.

Given that at least break-even voting strategies exist, the theory indicates that some get represented while others don't. There appears to be no great tendency for representatives to represent the entire district, unless, of course, the district is homogeneous. Within the theory a strategy of moderation, or an attempt to represent the whole district, might take the form of voting $(.5 + \epsilon)$ with the stronger group and $(.5 - \epsilon)$ with the weaker group. Actually the preceding is the case, except that the ϵ's are rather large. For a maximizer, $\epsilon = .5$. For a maintainer, $\epsilon \leqslant .5$. Thus, those who belong to the weaker group or set of groups have a definite tendency to get the short end of the stick.

Interestingly, we found no tendency for a representative's voting to respond monotonically to group strength. Nor did we find that electoral competition exerts a moderating influence on roll-call voting behavior. In agreement with traditional arguments, the theory indicates that a closely divided constituency puts the representative in a tight spot. But contrary to traditional arguments, both theory and data indicate that the representative does not gravitate to a spot midway between the two sides. Rather, he appears to go with one side or the other.

Specific findings aside, the theory indicates that the representative responds to *someone*. In other words, he is not a free agent. He has a "constituency" that he represents, although his constituency may not include the whole district, a majority of voters, or even a morally admirable minority.[b] The groups in the representative's constituency will be those he perceives as having the greatest potential to affect his reelection probability.

Perhaps we should emphasize that the stronger group or set of groups need not be a majority. In the extreme, the stronger group could be one individual—if the representative perceives him as the actor capable of affecting p the most. A small group which controls resources vital to an election campaign could receive excellent representation while the unorganized masses receive none. We may feel that in some situations our work amounts to a theory of corrupt representation, but certainly, there are corrupt representatives. We wish to explain their behavior, too.

A second major set of implications consists of those which involve the c_j estimates. These theoretical implications state that always in the one-group case and in the multigroup case with equal c_j's, the probability estimate that a vote will become a campaign issue does not affect a representative's choice of strategy, so long as these estimates are nonzero. If true, these implications are

[b]Fenno makes this point very strongly. After traveling with a sample of Congressmen, Fenno has concluded that one should distinguish four constituencies within the district. These are primary, party, policy, and style. Naturally, varying degrees of overlap may be present. Richard Fenno, personal conversations, 1971.

probably the most significant of the theory. They indicate that an informed, issue conscious citizenry (in the best traditions of democratic theory) may not be crucially important for representative government. The entire district need not be watching, just some part of it—a potential challenger, newspaper editor, interest group, or lone, informed citizen. Nor need they be watching at the time of the vote; just so they dig up the dirt before the election.

The American voter has taken a terrible beating from empirical political science. Supposedly, he is ignorant of the great issues of the day, apathetic, unaware of the candidates, unknowing even of which party is responsible for his present situation.[1] Understandably, many political scientists have expressed pessimistic judgments about representative government under such circumstances.[2] But our theoretical findings lead us to sympathize with Schattschneider's salvo:

One implication of public opinion studies ought to be resisted by all friends of freedom and democracy; the implication that democracy is a failure because the people are too ignorant to answer intelligently all the questions asked by the pollsters. This is a professorial invention for imposing professorial standards on the political system and deserves to be treated with extreme suspicion. Only a pedagogue would suppose that the people must pass some kind of examination to qualify for participation in a democracy. Who, after all, are these self-appointed censors who assume that they are in a position to flunk the whole human race? Their attitude would be less presumptuous if they could come up with a list of things that people must know. Who can say what the man on the street must know about public affairs?[3]

If the average voter is an ignoramus, why do investigators produce evidence which seemingly links electoral support to activities in office? V.O. Key, Jr., points out the association between policy preferences and switches in support of Presidential candidates.[4] Richard Boyd relates the parties' stands on the issues and their gain or loss in expected vote.[5] And of course, we have the Miller and Stokes "paradox" quoted in Chapter 2:

Of our sample of Congressmen who were opposed for re-election in 1958, more than four-fifths said the outcome in their districts had been strongly influenced by the electorate's response to their records and personal standing. Indeed, this belief is clear enough to present a notable contradiction: Congressmen feel that their individual legislative actions may have considerable impact on the electorate, yet some simple facts about the Representative's salience to his constituents imply that this could hardly be true.[6]

How does one reconcile findings which point simultaneously to voter ignorance and electoral accountability? At least part of the answer may inhere in the way in which a representative decides.[7] What counts is the *potential* damage of a vote. Even if only one in a hundred realize that potential, that may be the vote that ends a political life. Granted, the overwhelming bulk of Congressmen are reelected. But, by the same token, never does a Congressional election pass without leaving one or more Representatives and/or Senators consigned to political oblivion. There is always an example or two of a misstep that wiped out a political career. The costs of defeat are so enormous that the probability of defeat pales by comparison. Choosing discretion over valor, the representative votes as if the probability of his action becoming a campaign issue is unity.

Thus, if the theory is empirically accurate, we can take a more sanguine attitude toward the findings of public opinion studies. When confronted with impressive demonstrations of voter ignorance, we can shrug our shoulders and ask "so what?"[c] Only if public opinion studies show that *no one is watching ever*, do we have cause for despair.

In sum, then, the theory presented in the preceding pages indicates some reason for optimism on the part of those who value representative government. The findings of largely atheoretical empirical studies perhaps are not as damaging to the fact of electoral accountability as common-sense reasoning might lead one to expect. Instead, in a world of uncertainty, representatives may find it rational to act as if constituents were watching, mass constituency ignorance to the contrary notwithstanding.

Of course, we are arguing from an untested theory. Still, it is a theory that squares with the basic fact that representatives themselves believe in the visibility and importance of their records, a fact the quantitative studies find hard to accommodate. The theory embodies what we consider a necessary condition for understanding representative's roll-call voting: the constituency gives, and the constituency takes away. A student of representation who ignores that condition runs a high risk of misperceiving the representative process in the United States.

Notes

1. Philip Converse, "The Nature of Belief Systems in Mass Publics," in David Apter (ed.), *Ideology and Discontent* (New York: Free Press, 1964), pp. 206-261. Stokes and Miller, "Party Government and the Saliency of Congress."

2. Thomas Dye and Harmon Zeigler, for example, conclude that the hope for representative government depends primarily on the beneficence of elites rather than the power of the citizenry. See their *The Irony of Democracy* (Belmont, Calif.: Duxbury, 1970).

3. E.E. Schattschneider, *The Semi-Sovereign People* (New York: Holt, Rinehart and Winston, 1960), p. 135.

4. Key, *The Responsible Electorate*.

5. Richard Boyd, "Popular Control of Public Policy: A Normal Vote Analysis of the 1968 Election," *American Political Science Review*, 66 (1972), 429-449.

6. Miller and Stokes, "Constituency Influence in Congress," p. 48.

[c]Providing, of course, that the equal c_j assumption is usually approximately accurate.

7. Another part of the answer may be that voter ignorance has been overstated. A number of "revisionist" articles have been appearing in recent years. These studies raise questions about survey question wording, the apolitical nature of the American citizenry during the 1950s and the attention to concepts like "ideology" and "belief system" rather than more narrowly defined "issue publics." See David RePass, "Issue Salience and Party Choice," *American Political Science Review*, 65 (1971), 389-400. Gerald Pomper, "From Confusion to Clarity: Issues and American Voters, 1956-1968," *American Political Science Review*, 66 (1972), 415-428. Everett Ladd and Charles Hadley, "The American Party Coalitions: Patterns in Differentiation by Issues," 1972 APSA Paper. Peter Natchez and Irvin Bupp, "Candidates, Issues and Voting," *Public Policy*, 1 (1968), 409-437.

Bibliography

Bibliography

Anderson, Lee. "Individuality in Voting in Congress: A Research Note." *Midwest Journal of Political Science*, 8, 1964, 425-429.

Anderson, Lee F., Watts, Meredith W., Jr., and Wilcox, Allen R. *Legislative Roll-Call Analysis*. Evanston, Illinois: Northwestern University Press, 1966.

Aranson, Peter and Ordeshook, Peter. "Spatial Strategies for Sequential Elections," in Richard Niemi and Herbert Weisberg (eds.), *Probability Modeling in Political Science*. Columbus: Merrill, 1972.

Axelrod, Robert. *Conflict of Interest*. Chicago: Markham, 1970.

Barkley, Alben. *That Reminds Me*. Garden City, N.Y.: Doubleday, 1954.

Barry, Brian. *Sociologists, Economists and Democracy*. London: Collier-Macmillan, 1970.

Bauer, Raymond, Pool, Ithiel DeSola and Dexter, Lewis A. *American Business and Public Policy*. New York: Atherton, 1968.

Bendiner, Robert. *Obstacle Course on Capitol Hill*. New York: McGraw-Hill, 1946.

Black, Gordon. *Parties, Elections, and Public Opinion*. New York: Worth, forthcoming 1973.

Bolling, Richard. *Power in the House*. New York: Dutton, 1968.

Boyd, Richard. "Popular Control of Public Policy: A Normal Vote Analysis of the 1968 Election." *American Political Science Review*, 66, 1972, 429-449.

Buchanan, James and Tullock, Gordon. *The Calculus of Consent*. Ann Arbor: University of Michigan Press, 1962.

Burns, James M. *The Deadlock of Democracy*. Englewood Cliffs, New Jersey: Prentice-Hall, 1963.

Cell, Donald. "Maximizing, Satisficing, and Discretionary Power in Government." Paper presented to the Annual Meeting of the Public Choice Society, Blacksburg, Virginia, 1971.

Cherryholmes, Cleo and Shapiro, Michael. *Representatives and Roll Calls: A Computer Simulation of Voting in the Eighty-Eighth Congress*. Indianapolis: Bobbs-Merrill, 1968.

Clapp, Charles. *The Congressman: His Job As He Sees It*. Washington: Brookings Institution, 1963.

Clausen, Aage. *How Congressmen Decide: A Policy Focus*. New York: St. Martin's Press, 1973.

_____. "State Party Influence on Congressional Policy Decisions." *Midwest Journal of Political Science*, 16, 1972, 77-101.

Congressional Quarterly Service. *Congressional Quarterly Almanac*. Washington, D.C.: Congressional Quarterly Inc., annual.

_____. *Congressional Quarterly Census Analysis*. Washington, D.C.: Congressional Quarterly Inc., 1964.

Congressional Quarterly Service. *Congressional Quarterly Weekly Report.* Washington, D.C.: Congressional Quarterly Inc.

Converse, Philip. "The Nature of Belief Systems in Mass Publics," in David Apter (ed.), *Ideology and Discontent.* New York: The Free Press, 1964, 206-261.

Converse, Philip, Clausen, Aage, and Miller, Warren. "Electoral Myth and Reality: The 1964 Election." *American Political Science Review*, 59, 1965, 321-336.

Crane, Wilder. "Do Representatives Represent?" *Journal of Politics*, 22, 1960, 295-299.

Crane, Wilder and Watts, Meredith. *State Legislative Systems.* Englewood Cliffs, N.J.: Prentice-Hall, 1968.

Dahl, Robert. *A Preface to Democratic Theory.* Chicago: University of Chicago Press, 1956.

Davidson, Roger. *The Role of the Congressman.* New York: Pegasus, 1969.

Dexter, Lewis. "The Representative and His District." *Human Organization*, 16, 1947, 2-13.

Downs, Anthony. *An Economic Theory of Democracy.* New York: Harper and Row, 1957.

Dye, Thomas. "A Comparison of Constituency Influences in the Upper and Lower Chambers of a State Legislature." *Western Political Quarterly*, 14, June 1961, 473-480.

Dye, Thomas and Zeigler, Harmon. *The Irony of Democracy.* Belmont, California: Duxbury, 1970.

Erikson, Robert. "The Electoral Impact of Congressional Roll Call Voting." *American Political Science Review*, 65, 1971, 1018-1032.

Eulau, Heinz. "Changing Views of Representation," in Ithiel de Sola Pool (ed.), *Contemporary Political Science.* New York: McGraw-Hill, 1967, 53-85.

_____ . "The Ecological Basis of Party Systems: The Case of Ohio." *Midwest Journal of Political Science*, 1, 1957, 125-135.

Fenno, Richard. *Congressmen in Committees.* Boston: Little, Brown, 1973.

Flinn, Thomas. "Party Responsibility in the States: Some Causal Factors." *American Political Science Review*, 58, 1964, 60-71.

Flinn, Thomas and Wolman, Harold. "Constituency and Roll Call Voting: The Case of Southern Democratic Congressmen." *Midwest Journal of Political Science*, 10, 1966, 192-199.

Friedrich, Carl. *Man and His Government.* New York: McGraw-Hill, 1963.

Froman, Lewis. *Congressmen and Their Constituencies.* Chicago: Rand-McNally, 1963.

_____ . "The Importance of Individuality in Voting in Congress." *Journal of Politics*, 25, 1963, 324-332.

_____ ."Inter-Party Constituency Differences and Congressional Voting Behavior." *American Political Science Review*, 57, 1963, 57-61.

Gage, N.L. and Shimberg, B. "Measuring Senatorial Progressivism." *Journal of Abnormal and Social Psychology*, 44, 1949, 112-117.

Goldberg, Arthur. "Social Determinism and Rationality as Bases of Party Identification." *American Political Science Review*, 63, 1969.

_____. "A Theoretical Approach to Political Stability." American Political Science Association Paper, Washington, D.C., 1968.

Gregory, Roy. "Local Elections and the 'Rule of Anticipated Reactions'," *Political Studies*, 17, 1969, 31-47.

Groennings, Sven, Kelley, E.W., and Leiserson, Michael. *The Study of Coalition Behavior.* New York: Holt, Rinehart and Winston, 1970.

Harris, Richard. "Annals of Politics: How the People Feel." *New Yorker*, July 10, 1971, 48.

Heard, Alexander (ed.) *State Legislatures in American Politics.* Englewood-Cliffs, N.J.: Prentice-Hall, 1966.

Huntington, Samuel. "A Revised Theory of American Party Politics." *American Political Science Review*, 44, 1950, 669-677.

Irwin, F.W. "Stated Expectations as Functions of Probability and Desirability of Outcomes." *Journal of Personality*, 21, 1953, 329-335.

Jackson, John. "Some Indirect Evidences of Constituency Pressures on Senators." *Public Policy*, 16, 1967, 253-270.

_____. "Statistical Models of Senate Roll Call Voting." *American Political Science Review*, 65, 1971, 451-470.

Jewell, Malcolm and Patterson, Samuel. *The Legislative Process in the United States.* New York: Random House, 1966.

Keefe, William. "The Functions and Powers of the State Legislatures," in Alexander Heard (ed.), *State Legislatures in American Politics.* The American Assembly: Columbia University, 1966, 37-69.

Keefe, William and Ogul, Morris. *The American Legislative Process.* Englewood Cliffs, N.J.: Prentice-Hall, 2nd ed., 1968.

Kendall, Wilmoore and Carey, George. "The Intensity Problem and Democratic Theory." *American Political Science Review*, 62, 1968, 5-24.

Kessel, John. *The Goldwater Coalition.* Indianapolis: Bobbs-Merrill, 1968.

_____. "The Washington Congressional Delegation." *Midwest Journal of Political Science*, 8, 1964, 1-21.

Key, V.O., Jr. *Politics, Parties and Pressure Groups.* New York: Crowell, 5th ed., 1964.

_____. *The Responsible Electorate.* New York: Vintage, 1966.

Kingdon, John. *Candidates For Office: Beliefs and Strategies.* New York: Random House, 1966.

Koehler, David and Oshel, Robert. "Electoral Margins and Legislative Voting Power: A Test of the Relationship Between Electoral Strategies and Legislative Effectiveness." Public Choice Society Paper, College Park, Maryland, 1973.

Kyburg, Henry E., Jr. and Smokler, Howard E. *Studies in Subjective Probability.* New York: Wiley, 1964.

Ladd, Everett and Hadley, Charles. "The American Party Coalitions: Patterns in

Differentiation by Issues." American Political Science Association Paper, 1972.

LeBlanc, Hugh. "Voting in State Senates: Party and Constituency Influences." *Midwest Journal of Political Science*, 13, 1969, 33-57.

Lockard, Duane. *New England State Politics.* Princeton: Princeton University Press, 1959.

Luce, R.D. and Shipley, E.F. "Preference Probability Between Gambles as a Step Function of Event Probability." *Journal of Experimental Psychology*, 63, 1962, 42-49.

MacRae, Duncan. *Dimensions of Congressional Voting.* Berkeley: University of California Press, 1958.

_____ . *Issues and Parties in Legislative Voting.* New York: Harper and Row, 1970.

_____ . "The Relation Between Roll-Call Votes and Constituencies in the Massachusetts House of Representatives." *American Political Science Review*, 46, 1952, 1046-1055.

Matthews, Donald and Stimson, James. "Decision-Making by U.S. Representatives: A Preliminary Model," in S. Sidney Ulmer (ed.), *Political Decision-Making.* New York: Van Nostrand, 1970, 14-43.

Mayhew, David. *Party Loyalty Among Congressmen.* Cambridge: Harvard University Press, 1966.

McClosky, Herbert, Hoffman, Paul and O'Hara, Rosemary. "Issue Conflict and Consensus Among Party Leaders and Followers." *American Political Science Review*, 54, 1960, 406-427.

McKelvey, Richard D. "Policy Related Voting and its Effects on Electoral Equilibrium: A Reformulation and Generalization of Some Theorems on Abstention in Spatial Models of Party Competition." American Political Science Association Convention Paper, Washington, D.C., 1972.

McKelvey, Richard and Richelson, Jeff. "Cycles of Risk." Public Choice Society Paper, College Park, Maryland, 1973.

Michel, Jerry and Dillehay, Ronald. "Reference Behavior Theory and the Elected Representative." *Western Political Quarterly*, 22, 1969, 759-773.

Miller, Warren. "Majority Rule and the Representative System of Government," in E. Allardt and Stein Rokkan (eds.), *Mass Politics.* New York: Free Press, 1970, 284-311.

Miller, Warren E. and Stokes, Donald E. "Constituency Influence in Congress," in Robert Peabody and Nelson Polsby (eds.), *New Perspectives on the House of Representatives.* Chicago: Rand McNally, 1969, 31-54.

Natchez, Peter and Bupp, Irvin. "Candidates, Issues and Votes." *Public Policy*, 1, 1968, 409-437.

New York Times. 10 April 1970, 1, 42. 20 April 1970, 63. 23 April 1970, 36. 5 June 1970, 40. 4 November 1970, 19. 5 November 1970, 43.

Northrup, F.S.C. *The Logic of the Sciences and Humanities.* Cleveland: Meridian Books, 1947.

Olson, Mancur. *The Logic of Collective Action.* New York: Schocken, 1968.

Ordeshook, Peter. "Extensions to a Model of the Electoral Process and Implications for the Theory of Responsible Parties." *Midwest Journal of Political Science*, 14, 1970, 43-70.

Parsons, Malcolm. "Quasi-Partisan Conflict in a One-Party Legislative System: The Florida Senate, 1947-1961." *American Political Science Review*, 56, 1962, 605-614.

Patterson, Samuel. *Labor Lobbying and Labor Reform: The Passage of the Landrum-Griffin Act.* Indianapolis: Bobbs-Merrill, 1966.

_____ . "The Role of the Deviant in the State Legislative System: The Wisconsin Assembly." *Western Political Quarterly*, 14, 1961, 460-473.

_____ . "Dimensions of Voting Behavior in a One-Party State Legislature." *Public Opinion Quarterly*, 26, 1962, 185-201.

Pesonen, Pertti. "Close and Safe State Elections in Massachusetts." *Midwest Journal of Political Science*, 7, 1963, 54-70.

Pitkin, Hanna (ed.) *Representation.* New York: Atherton Press, 1969.

Polsby, Nelson. "The Labyrinth: A Bill Becomes a Law," in *Congress and the Presidency.* Englewood Cliffs, N.J.: Prentice-Hall, 1964, 62-81.

Pomper, Gerald. "From Confusion to Clarity: Issues and American Voters, 1956-1968." *American Political Science Review*, 66, 1972, 415-428.

Rabushka, Alvin and Shepsle, Kenneth. *Politics in Plural Societies: A Theory of Democratic Instability.* Columbus: Charles E. Merrill, 1972.

Rae, Douglas and Taylor, Michael. *The Analysis of Political Cleavages.* New Haven: Yale University Press, 1970.

Raiffa, Howard. *Decision Analysis.* Reading, Mass.: Addison-Wesley, 1968.

Ranney, Austin. *The Doctrine of Responsible Party Government.* Urbana: University of Illinois Press,1954.

RePass, David. "Issue Salience and Party Choice." *American Political Science Review*, 65, 1971, 389-400.

Riker, William. *The Theory of Political Coalitions.* New Haven: Yale University Press, 1962.

Savage, Leonard. *The Foundations of Statistics.* New York: Wiley, 1954.

Schattschneider, E.E. *The Semi-Sovereign People.* New York: Holt, Rinehart and Winston, 1960.

Schlaifer, Robert. *Analysis of Decisions Under Uncertainty.* New York: McGraw-Hill, 1967.

Shannon, Wayne. *Party, Constituency and Congressional Voting.* Baton Rouge: Louisiana State University Press, 1968.

Simon, Herbert. *Models of Man.* New York: Wiley, 1957.

Smith, Frank. *Congressman From Mississippi.* New York: Pantheon Books, 1964.

Sorauf, Frank J. *Party Politics in America.* Boston: Little, Brown, 1968.

Stokes, Donald and Miller, Warren. "Party Government and the Saliency of Congress." *Public Opinion Quarterly*, 26, 1962, 531-546.

Stone, Clarence. "Issue Cleavage Between Democrats and Republicans in the United States House of Representatives." *Journal of Public Law*, 14, 1965, 343-358.

Sullivan John. "Political Correlates of Social, Economic and Religious Diversity in the American States. *Journal of Politics*, 35, 1973, 73.

Sullivan, John and O'Connor, Robert. "Electoral Choice and Popular Control of Public Policy: The Case of the 1966 House Elections." *American Political Science Review*, 64, 1972, 1256-1268.

Turner, Julius. *Party and Constituency: Pressures on Congress.* Baltimore: The Johns Hopkins Press, 1951.

Turner, Julius and Schneier, Edward. *Party and Constituency: Pressures on Congress.* Baltimore: The Johns Hopkins Press, rev. ed., 1970.

Van Der Slik, Jack. "Roll Call Voting in the House of Representatives of the 88th Congress: Constituency Characteristics and Party Affiliation." Public Affairs Research Bureau, Southern Illinois University, 1969.

Index

Index

Abortion, votes on, 45
Absences at roll call, 113
Abstention rates and abstainers, 69-72, 78-79, 112-117
Activism, party, 110-111
Age, voting, 14, 84
Agrarian districts, 22
Agriculture: assistance for, 12-15
Aid: agricultural, 13-15; foreign, 12-15, 66; educational, 13
Alabama, 97
Alford, Dale, cited, 45n
Allardt, E., cited, 8
Amendments to bills, 82
AFL-CIO, support from, 65n, 111
American Political Science Review, 10, 18n, 21, 121
An Economic Theory of Democracy (Downs), 20
Analysis of Political Cleavages, The (Taylor), 55n
Anticipated reaction, law of, 32
Antilabor, positions of, 62
Apathy of constitutents, 32
Authority, appeals to, 91
Arkansas, 45n, 97
Aspirations, levels of, 38
Assembly-line workers, 111
Assumption: additive, 81; motivational, 35-38, 40
Attitudes, 109-111; personal policy, 7-8
Attitudinal heterogeneity, 91, 94
Attitudinal homogeneity, 98-99
Atypical hypothesis, 4-7, 11

Banks, data, 24
Barkley, Alben, cited, 39
Bayesian decision theory, 30, 34
Behavior: hypotheses, 37-39; irrational, 61; of maintainers, 58-59; nonrational, 61; patterns of, 61; voting, 12-15, 40, 50, 53-54, 64, 72, 100, 122
Bias, rural, 91
Black belt district, 13, 34
Blacks, voter registration of, 31, 46, 81, 91
Blue collar workers, 17, 64-65
Bollings, Richard, cited, 3n

Bonjean, Charles, cited, 41n
Boyd, Richard, cited, 123
Burns, J.M., cited, 91
Businesses, large and small, 31, 81, 91-92

California, 97
Campaigns, election, 32, 111; issues in, 55, 113, 122; workers in, 84
Candidates, marginal, 22, 92
Canned statistical packages, 24
Capitalism, 93
Caring, probability of, 55
Catholicism and Catholic districts, 31, 45, 81
Census, Bureau of, 17, 66
Citizenry, informed, 123
Civil liberties, voting on, 13-15
Civil Rights, issue of, 7-9, 19, 45-46, 66, 96, 108
Civil Rights Act of 1957, 34
Clapp, Charles, cited, 32
Classical thinkers, ideas of, 1
Clausen, Aage, cited, 13-15, 17, 32
"Close" districts, 5-6
Clustering techniques, 12
Coalition dynamics, theory of, 81
Colorado, 97, 104
Comparisons, cross-district, 107
Communications, 85
Competition: of districts, 6-8, 11, 92, 100-101; dynamics of, 11n, 20; electoral, 4, 91, 100, 103, 110; party, 91-92, 100-101; safe, 90
Compromise positions, 54, 106, 111
Computers, facilities for, 24
Conformity, pressures for, 91
Configuration, 43, 91
Conflictual constituency districts, 49-63, 69, 76-80, 90, 112
Congress: of 1921, 3; of 1931, 3; of 1937, 3; of 1944, 3; 81st, 12; 82nd, 13; 83rd, 13; 84th, 13, 103; 85th, 13, 18, 116-117; 86th, 7, 12-13, 102-103; 87th, 7, 12-13, 102-103; 88th, 13, 65n, 103-104, 116-117; 89th, 102, 104, 107-108; 90th, 102, 104-105, 107-108; 91st, 13, 117
Congressional Democratic Party, 10

137

About the Author

Morris P. Fiorina is assistant professor of political science in the Division of the Humanities and Social Sciences and the Environmental Quality Laboratory at the California Institute of Technology. He received the B.A. with honors in political science from Allegheny College, where he was elected to Phi Beta Kappa. He received the M.A. and the Ph.D. in political science from the University of Rochester, where he was the recipient of a New York State Herbert Lehman Fellowship. Dr. Fiorina has contributed articles to *American Politics Quarterly, American Political Science Review,* and *Behavioral Science.*